FUNDAMENTALS

OF

SOCIAL RESEARCH

FUNDAMENTALS OF SOCIAL RESEARCH

Lokesh K. Prasad

Delta Book World
New Delhi-110 002

ISBN: 978-93-85719-40-0
First Published in 2021

Published by **Abhishek Goel** on behalf of

Delta Book World
G-4, Prahlad House
4832/24, Ansari Road
New Delhi - 110 002 (India)

Tel.: 011-4707 2321
E-mail: deltabookworld@gmail.com
Website: www.kaveribooks.com

PRINTED IN INDIA

Dedicated To

My Father
(Late) Professor R. C. Prasad
(1934-1983)

&

My Father-in-law
(Late) Shri Susanta Kumar Roy
(1942-2017)

Preface

The 'Fundamentals of Social Research' is an attempt to introduce researchers engaged in the study of human activity and society with the ways how to arrive at sociological inquiry based on validated facts. For any research to have scientific fervour, researchers need to know about the methods or ways to attain it which is possible with their in-depth knowledge of the subject in which they are involved in. So this book covers the ideas of prominent social thinkers from the sixteenth century up to the present to provide an evolutionary perspective of human thought in social research. The purpose is to analyze the intellectual trajectory of social research which kept evolving with the change in the prevailing socio-politico-economic conditions.

The proficiency in research methodologies and methods provides its learners an asset which is helpful in term of job opportunities for those who aim to make their career in any field that requires understanding social reality, such as, market research, public opinion poll, communication studies, advertisement, book publishing, media studies, political party propaganda, public administration, development projects administration and implementation, personnel management, labour studies, civil society organizations and a host of others who require knowledge and skills for pursuing research degrees like M.Phil. and Ph.D. in social sciences.

The global spread of industrialism coupled with technological revolution in the field of communications has vastly expanded the scope of social research. At most levels in one's career, understanding social reality provides the ability to hold on to one's job, to succeed in getting further promotions, and above all, to effectively participate in decision-making processes that exist in all jobs. There is currently a growing professional and commercial demand for graduates who have qualifications to carry out social research.

All attempts to make social research scientifically valid involve clarity of perspectives or orientations that guide one's quest for collection of facts and all such clarity is worthwhile only when it accompanies scientific methods and techniques of collecting, analyzing and interpreting facts.

Lokesh K. Prasad

16th June 2021
New Delhi

Contents

Part IV
Methodological Guidelines for Social Research

Introduction

Humankind has a tendency to explore and understand the world around them. It is very common these days for a large section of humanity to look for explanations that are scientific. But at one time such explanations brought the wrath of the authorities, usually religious authority. As science made increasing strides revealing in turn the mystery of nature over which humankind tried to rule, the methodologies employed by the natural and physical sciences came to rule as what should be the best methods of acquiring knowledge. All philosophy originates from the basic sense of wonder humankind experience and that this sense of wonder that lead to different explanations or theories. It is, therefore, not surprising that on the question of knowledge there are several contesting viewpoints.

For a long historical time, the advocates of logic had to fight with the domination of religion to establish the supremacy of human reason and mind over the supernatural domain or the will of God. They advocated that society is not a creation of God governed by a divine will but a creation of human beings and an entity that has an objective and changing existence that can be studied from the outside. They projected certain basic premises regarding the truth of social existence. These were in the form of a universal history, holding a basic supposition that all societies are evolved and have gone through various transformations to be what they are today; an idea of progress that things are going towards betterment and the triumph of reason is the ultimate goal of humankind.

This criticality was not necessarily negative in nature. The Enlightenment was progressive and spoke of the primacy of reason.

It did not oppose the ethical and spiritual core of Christianity. It opposed only the closed and dogmatic character of Christianity and provided the foundations of a new world based on a secular and liberal worldview. In other words, the roots of modernity: a project that celebrates scientificity, rationality and individuality could be found in the Enlightenment agenda itself. This intellectual movement in Europe believed in a linear and historical progress which gave a new dynamism to the exploration of knowledge, innovation and experimentation. It fought a great battle against the Church, particularly its implicit notion of originals and imperfectability. Hence, their agenda was future-oriented and optimistic. Since the seventeenth century up to the nineteenth century, the main epistemological positions or theories of knowledge which dominated the philosophical inquiry into understanding the social reality were rationalism, empiricism, idealism and positivism.

What made Auguste Comte immortal in the discipline was his celebrated 'law of three stages'. To comprehend the deeper meaning of these three stages of law, imagine fire as a phenomenon. It is possible to explain it, as the Vedic hymns suggest, as a manifestation of a powerful deity called *Agni*. Now Comte would have argued that explaining fire as a manifestation of *Agni* is a theological explanation. But suppose one goes beyond these Vedic rituals, and enters a higher stage of contemplative and abstract thought, and sees fire as something symbolizing human beings, quest for truth and purity: burning all egotistic passions and impulses. Yes, Comte would have argued that it is a metaphysical explanation. But then, if we argue that fire is just a physico-chemical phenomenon that can be explained in the form of a natural law, Comte would have argued that we have finally arrived at the positive stage. In other words, positivist knowledge is empirical and universal; something that is concrete and demonstrable. It demystifies the world. So when we see the rains, we need not explain it as *Indra's* blessing; nor do you see it as a manifestation of man's poetry to overcome the dryness of his being. Instead, the rains we see, in this positivist stage, can be explained in terms of the scientific principles of heat, cloud formation and water cycle. The entire phenomenon can be understood better if we reflect on the self-perception of science. For instance, it is argued that science is a radical departure from common sense (Nagel 1971: 1-14). Well, common sense may not necessarily be false. But common sense, unlike science, is seldom accompanied by a search for systematic explanations derived from solid factual evidence. For instance, before the advent of modern science people knew the function of the wheel. But it was only modern science that provided us with an explanatory principle like the frictional force to make sense of the operation of wheels. Likewise, the principles formulated by Newton could explain innumerable facts: the behaviour of the tides, the paths of projectiles, and the moon's motion. It is also argued that, unlike the indeterminacy of common sense, the language of science is more specific, focused and pointed. It abhors all sorts of vagueness. Even though the poets may speak of infinite stars, it would be argued, astronomers are interested in calculating and measuring their exact number. Furthermore, science, unlike common sense, is a distant, detached and abstract exercise. Whereas common sense has an intimate relationship with our everyday world, science is essentially neutral. We may enjoy the colour of the sunset: but then, the electromagnetic theory, which provides a systematic account of optical phenomena, retains its remoteness and abstraction. In fact, science deliberately neglects the immediate values of things. That is why it is argued that science is primarily critical in spirit. Whereas common sense tends to take things for granted, science problematizes even our most cherished beliefs. This does not mean that common sense is necessarily false and science is true. What distinguishes science is its critical spirit, its insistence on empirical evidence. Nagel writes;

> "The difference between the cognitive claims of science and common sense, which stems from the fact that the former are the products of the scientific method, does not connote that the former are invariably true. It does follow that while common sense beliefs are usually accepted without a critical evaluation of the evidence available, the evidence for the conclusions of science conforms to standards such that a significant proportion of conclusions supported by similar structured evidence remains in good agreement with additional factual data when fresh data are obtained" (1971: 13).

Modern science was evolving, arousing immense optimism and becoming hegemonic. The scientific thinking emanating from Bacon, Descartes and Newton, and scientific inventions and discoveries were altering the cultural and intellectual landscape of Europe. And eventually, the Enlightenment in the eighteenth century was a turning point. Voltaire believed that human beings were neither good nor evil as such; instead, the specificity of circumstances would matter a great deal in unfolding the potential of human beings. In other words, it is possible for human beings to shape their destiny and create a better world. Its optimism was sustained by its epistemology: its spirit of critical enquiry. "Our age is in a special degree", Immanuel Kant wrote, "the age of criticism, and to criticism everything must submit." Nothing was, therefore, taken for granted. This criticality gave a new momentum, enabled humankind to come out of the trap of closed and dogmatic thinking, and finally revealed a positive relationship between reason and freedom, science and truth. It meant celebrating a new age of reason, objectivity and criticality. It was like coming out of the medieval order, religious influences, and asserting that scientific thinking would enable us to create a better world. It was difficult to escape the influence of the age. It was difficult not to be influenced by the spectacular success story of science. Science became knowledge itself: real, objective and foundational. And to survive in such a milieu was to accept science and its ascending power. Beginning with Galileo Galilei (1564-1642) and Isaac Newton (1642-1727) natural science began a conquest of the natural world, which was a staggering success. This success did not go unnoticed in the social sciences. Rather, as many commentators have noted, the social sciences were born in the shadow of these triumphs. Furthermore, the methodological lessons that the natural sciences were teaching seemed to be very clear: if the methods of the natural science are strictly adhered to, then the spectacular success of these sciences could be matched in the social sciences. The social sciences had only to await the arrival of their Newton (Hekman 1986: 5).

The assumption was that the identity of social science as "true knowledge" could not be established without adopting the method of the natural sciences. There was yet another important factor. The new age characterized by the Industrial Revolution, expanding trade and commerce, and emergent bourgeoisie altered power relations in the West. It was the time that witnessed the assertion of the new elite: technologists, scientists and capitalists. They saw immense possibilities in science, and were strong adherents of a positivistic/scientific culture and mode of enquiry. Yes, there were dissenting voices, say, the voices emanating from romanticism that critiqued the worship of science and reason, and pleaded for imagination, subjectivity and creativity But then, the language of science was irresistible. The politico-economic establishment was sustaining it. Science was going to stay, and positivism was its inevitable consequence.

Theory in the social sciences has continuously reflected changing social conditions as evident from the basic or major premises on which these theories are based. The premises are the given conditions or universal truths that we take for granted when we formulate a research problem or look for some explanations of a social phenomenon. In the early twentieth century the concept of change became a major theoretical and ethical issue as it was realized that change was an essential dimension of our lives. The two World Wars, the independence of the colonies, rapid industrialization and capitalist expansion all had a great influence on the theory of social research. Not only change but also conflict became a central concept in the social science research and it became increasingly debated as to what was a more natural human condition, harmony or conflict?

Until the ninety-sixties, the field of social research remained largely in the realm of functionalism with its roots in the writings of Auguste Comte. The prominent functionalist Talcott Parsons (1902-1979) attempted to provide a grand theory by generalizations about the nature of society and history. His work, *The Structure of Social Action* (1937), is one of the most influential theoretical works of the twentieth century. The functional theories of Malinowski (1944) and Radcliffe-Brown (1952) provided middle-range theories which were more inductive in nature and were built up around a limited set of observed facts. But they were criticized as not really reflecting social reality. Increasingly by the nineteen sixties criticism of functional approach was emerging that considered the homeostatic (the state of remaining at a constant level) system forming the basis of the functional theory as utopian. Some criticisms like those of Robert Merton (1968), Raymond Firth (1901-2002) and Edmund Leach (1910-1989) came out from within the limits of functionality. These critical views reinterpreted the concepts to introduce more flexibility. For example, Merton introduced the concepts of functional alternative, and functional substitutability. Similarly, Firth gave the concept of social organization and Leach analyzed the concept of dynamic equilibrium. The emphasis in all these was on a middle range of generalization.

Positivism persisted in theory in the period of what can be designated as 'high modernism' and is evident in the structuralism. In fact, structuralism emerged as an intellectual tradition in social theory. Like functionalism, it also derived its inspiration from Durkheim. While functionalism accepted the premises of biology, structuralism used linguistic models to explain social and cultural phenomena. Of the French structuralism, the works of Claude Levi-Strauss (1908-2009) have had a lasting impact on the social sciences. He extended the connection between structures of thought and the internal structure of the human brain borrowing from the theoretical principles of structural linguistics; that is to say, he applied the methods of structural linguistics to social phenomena.

A major turn away from functionalism was towards recognizing conflict as a central dimension of society. In post-nineteen-sixties, increasingly, the concept of society becomes defined in terms of conflict and competition rather than harmony and function. Power and individual and group interests overshadow cooperation and altruism as leading forces of society. The oppressive events of the twentieth century, the World Wars, the holocaust, the marginalization and genocide of colonial rule, Vietnam and Korea war, all combined to produce a critical approach to society where utopia was nowhere to be seen. Such theories like that of George Lukacs and Jurgen Habermas were highly contemplative and emphasized processes such as inter-subjectivity. They were deeply concerned with the dehumanizing processes taking place in the world and also the role of theory in obliterating the human dimension. Oppression and human struggles in various parts of the world often became central themes of analysis.

In the post-nineteen-seventies era, the recognition of the process of "construction" was contingent upon the process of deconstruction. The notions of deconstruction and destructuralization spread across all fields of humanities, literature and art. The fixed faith in the definition of knowledge as that generated by western science was challenged, so was the so-called "progress" embodied in western civilization. The entire notion that knowledge exists as "facts" that can be established with the help of western scientific methods, and even that there is a fixed “reality” out there, was criticized. The reason for this radical departure from modernism was the failure of western science and systems of knowledge to deliver the goods in a world threatened with environmental disasters, diseases such as AIDS, failure of civil society and deepening inequalities and injustice across the world. Another reason was the emergence of scholars from various race, class, ethnic, and gender categories. The central figure of the white and male scholar was displaced and taken over by a variety of others, who challenged the truth status of the findings. In the forefront were what was known as the colonial critique and the feminist critique. A new generation of scholars confronted the political and economic realities of ‘colonial knowledge’ by following the motivations and power equations involved in the production of such knowledge. But extreme reflexivity of post modernism itself was unable to depict the real basis of human inequality. The problems of diversity and providing a critique of human situations of real inequality, human suffering and exploitation are still valid theoretically well into the twenty-first century. Just before the emergence of post-modernism, further questioning and debating eventually saw the emergence of such schools of thought as phenomenology, hermeneutics, symbolic interactionism and ethnomethodology. Hence, the birth of modernity had given rise to both positivist tradition and interpretative tradition. As the later philosophers of science challenged the Enlightenment view of science, there were corresponding changes in the philosophy of social science. Karl Popper’s critical rationalism questioned positivistic certainties; and Thomas Kuhn’s notion of extraordinary science led to paradigm shifts and more innovative science. Paul Feyerabend’s critique of the hegemony of scientific method opened the way for plurality of knowledge systems, methods and traditions of enquiry. These developments in the philosophy of science showed the way to the research in social sciences for coming out of the shadow of the natural science.

In the present day context of globalization, culture and society are becoming more and more amorphous as concepts. Identities are no longer seen as closed and definitive but contested, discordant and constitutive of disparate elements picked up both locally and globally. Traditions are no longer viewed as given but as reinvented every time. Foucault’s denunciation of western forms of knowledge as an instrument of domination rather than an instrument of truth has dealt a blow to all that was sanctified in the name of science. Now science is no longer an objective system of truth but a regional form of knowledge that had sought to supersede all other forms of knowledge by acts of force rather than reason. For social scientists it has meant that one takes a fresh look at the creation of the research subject, noting the positions of inequality between observer and observed. This process of restructuring of truth has its biggest triumph in that subjects have the option of refashioning themselves and resist the imposition of anything in the name of normal or given. The acceptance of diversity and the rejection of inequality have been a major effort of contemporary theory, reflecting and striving for a better world. The call for active participation in the process of understanding and subsequently fashioning the social reality all around us is gaining recognition in the twenty-first century. In the social sciences there was a revival of evolution in the form of neo evolutionary theories, and in sociological research the work of Niklas Luhmann (1927-1998) emphasized the role of the environment in the study of social systems. In all such theories we see an attempt to get away from too much generalization to come back to more concrete and material conditions but at the same time not to forget the symbolic dimensions of human society. Both cultural ecology and Luhmann's (1998) general system's approach included environment as a variable for understanding social reality. Adaptation to environment became a key concept and mal-adaptation was introduced into analysis.

As evident, since the beginning of the 1990s, debates about globalization have succeeded and increasingly displaced arguments about 'post modernism.' It is not just about the expansion of free trade and competitiveness in a global market but involves a process of social change in which the local and the global world are mutually implicated. In other words, it refers to the social processes of 'time-space compression' in which the constraints of geography on social and cultural arrangements recede; and people become increasing aware that they recede. As a process, thus, globalization is typically defined, in economic terms, as "the closer integration of the countries and peoples of the world...by the enormous reduction of costs of transportation and communication, and breaking down of artificial barriers to the flow of goods, services, capital, knowledge and (to a lesser extent) people across borders." (Stiglitz 2002:9). As an organizing principle, it can be conceptualized as "deterritorization" (Scholte 2000:46), that is, as the explanations in accounting for contemporary social change, as "the 'lifting out' of social relations from local contexts of interaction and their restructuring across indefinite spans of time-space" (Giddens 1990: 21). The economic, political and cultural subsystems of societies are interconnected and interdependent as never before. Moreover, we are increasingly conscious of the world as a whole. The world 'shrinks' as immense flows of capital, money, goods, services, people information, technologies, policies, ideas, images and regulations transcend individual nation-states and dissolve their borders. Thus, the development of a capitalist world economy, a shifting system of nation-states and the rise of global culture are the salient features of contemporary globalization. However, global culture is ambiguous. Broadly, it involves the worldwide diffusion of capitalist cultural products and the spread of consumerist ideology, as well as the local interpretation and indigenization of those global cultural products.

In the natural sciences, as mentioned earlier, there is a clear separation between the researcher and the object of research whereas in the social sciences there is hardly any such separation. "The object of social sciences," Morgenthau writes, "is man, not as a product of nature but as both the creature and the creator of history in and through which his individuality and freedom of choice manifest themselves" (1955: 441). In the social sciences, there is a continuous attempt to come to grips with the influence of the subject on the object and with the impact of that influence on process of producing a valid knowledge. As Barnes argued, the distinctive quality of social science research is essentially located in the "activity in which human beings study themselves that complex ethical questions have to be faced as an abiding concomitant of that activity" (1977: 2). For him, ethical questions are "intrinsic, ubiquitous and unavoidable" in the social sciences (Ibid. 3). For this reason, the ethics of inquiry in social research has been a concern since its inception. And, it is this concern that brings about new methodologies or perspectives to understand the social phenomena around us. Hence, the ethical issues have remained a major difficult interest in any social research.

A Brief Overview

Part one of the book examines the natural science model as an ideal for the study of society. Various scholars have viewed differently on the status of social science in relation to the natural science. So the central questions we have discussed focus on the issue whether the study of humans and society is scientific in the same manner as the study of natural objects. Can we speak of a unified science, or should natural-science inquiry and social-science inquiry be viewed as two basically different activities? Can we think of "science of men" be different from natural science? Chapter two demonstrates the successes won by the scientific method in the seventeenth century fostered the growth of a more secular and rationalistic spirit in European society and helped to make the eighteenth century an "Age of Reason." It describes the beginnings of the modern science in the sixteenth and seventeenth centuries, the advances in mathematical method, and the brilliant discoveries in astronomy, physics, and other fields of investigation; how the scientific and intellectual character of our time as well as its technical achievements was a growth deep rooted in the whole course of Western civilization; how it has taken on a new quality with the dawn of the nuclear age, as humankind faces up to the fateful task of seeing to it that his destructive powers do not overbalance his constructive genius, that his control over natural forces does not outrun his control of himself and finally, how science with its central principles of objectivity, universalization and causal explanation did have a tremendous impact on the formation of modern social science research and its methodology.

Part two conceptualizes the main current of ideas put forward by philosophers from the seventeenth century up to the nineteenth century. From rationalism of Rene Descartes (1596-1650) and the 'idols of mind' of Francis Bacon (1561-1626), we have analysed the views of John Locke (1632-1704), David Hume (1711-1776), George Berkeley (1685-1753), Immanuel Kant (1724-1804), Saint Simon (1760-1825), Auguste Comte (1798-1857) and Emile Durkheim (1858-1917). They provided the philosophical basis to comprehend social phenomena and to engage in discovering new ways of seeing the social world.

Part three introduces us to a more formal and structured discussion of the theories put forward by contemporary social thinkers in order to understand social reality. Each chapter of the part is devoted to one of these contemporary theories, namely, functionalism, structuralism, critical theory, postmodernism, phenomenology, hermeneutics, symbolic interactionism and feminism and provides an exposition of the theory in question while pointing to problems, ambiguities, and defects. Although these chapters may be read independently of one another, together they unfold the central thesis of the book.

Part four seeks to provide methodological guidelines to researchers engaged the in the study of human activity and society. Chapter fifteen emphasises the role of observation and logic in understanding the social reality. Chapter sixteen deals with the rules of collection of data without any subjective understanding, preconceived notions or prejudices. Chapter seventeen is concerned with theory building in social research; purpose of concepts; scope of social research; and, how to keep away the entry of researcher's value in sociological research. Chapter eighteen deals with testing of hypothesis in social research. Chapter nineteen provides the insights to cope with diversities in social research.

Part I

Nature and Growth of Social Research

1

Nature of Social Research

In our discussion on the nature of social research the focus of analysis would be on the central questions, first, whether the study of human and society would be scientific in the same manner as the study of natural objects; second, can we speak of a unified science, or should natural-science inquiry and social-science inquiry be viewed as two basically different activities; and, third, is it possible to have a general social theory in social sciences which would consist of a set of general, testable, explanatory propositions applicable to the total area of collective human behaviour. But, the history of social research reveals that these questions were to be both difficult to answer and remained a matter of debate since its inception. The reason was that, besides having fundamental methodological consequences, these questions touch on sensitive factors such as the status of social science in relation to natural science (Flyvbjerg 2001: 25), as well as what Richard Bernstein calls, "Cartesian anxiety," that is, the fear of ending in relativism and nihilism when one departs from the analytical-rational scientific tradition that has dominated Western science since Descartes (Bernstein 1985: 16). Also, these questions involve the logical and epistemological problems of social science method disputed among philosophers of history.

Natural-Science Model: An Ideal Type for Social Science

The natural-science model has been an ideal type shared by several traditions in the study of human activity. During 18th century, Nicolas de Condorcet (1743-1794), a French philosopher, postulated that his descendants would surpass him in "wisdom as in enlightenment" acquiring a language "exact and precise," just as in natural sciences. In his *Outlines of an Historical View of the Progress of Human Mind*, he wrote,

> "Those sciences, created almost in our days, the object of which is man himself, the direct goal of which is the happiness of man, will enjoy a progress no less sure than that of the physical science, and this idea so sweet, that our descendants will surpass us in wisdom as in enlightenment, is no longer an illusion...one cannot help seeing that, as they are based like physical sciences, on the observation of fact, they must follow the same method, acquire a language equally exact and precise, attaining the same degree of certainty" (quoted in Scott 1998:9).

During nineteenth century, Condorcet's ideas were carried forward by Auguste Comte (1798-1857), Karl Marx (1818-1883), Sigmund Freud (1856-1939), and Emile Durkheim (1858-1917). They had faith in the natural-science model as an ideal type for the study of humans and society though with somewhat different notions of science in mind. Auguste Comte in his book, *Course of Positive Philosophy* wrote, "Like scientists who studied the natural world and discovered the nature of laws determining the behaviour of matter in the physical world, it was possible to discover the laws which determined the behaviour of people in the social world." He stated that the laws governing the behaviour of people in the social world could be discovered through the development of a positive philosophy of human social development. For him, the social world was as regular and objective as was the natural world. According to him, social scientists could use the methodology and insight of the natural sciences as the model for the development social physics. He believed that social laws governed the social world just as natural laws governed the natural world.

In *Paris Manuscripts*, Karl Marx expressed his faith in a future unified science. According to him, "natural science will in time subsume the science of man just as the science of man will subsume natural science: there will be one science" (1975:355). He was profoundly influenced by Newton (1642-1727) and Darwin (1809-1882); he dedicated his second volume of *Capital* (1867) to Charles Darwin. His "scientificity" was seen in his urge to discover the 'iron laws' of capitalist development. For this, he pleaded for universal generalizations like 'the history of hitherto existing societies is the history of class struggle'. Distinguishing between ideology and historical materialism, he opined, the former distorts and falsifies the reality, whereas latter enables us to see the reality as it is, that is to say, how the mode of production seeks to govern the socio-cultural life and resultant conflicts and contradictions in society.

Sigmund Freud, too, early in his career was as optimistic as the young Marx. His declared goal was "to furnish a psychology that shall be a natural science, that is, to represent psychical processes as quantitatively determinate states of specifiable material particles, thus making those processes perspicuous and free from contradiction" (Freud 1950: 295). Later on, he continued to view the natural sciences as an ideal worth striving for, but he became more sceptical about how far one could go in approaching this ideal within psychology and psychiatry. "I always envy the physicists and mathematicians who can stand on firm ground," he later said, "I hover, so to speak, in the air. Mental events seem to be immeasurable and probably always will be so" (quoted in Clark 1982: 470).

For Emile Durkheim, sociological explanations are objective and independent and cannot be reduced into psychological terms. It was in this sense that Durkheim made an interesting point that "a whole is not identical with the sum of its parts" (1964: 102). In his opinion, it acquires an independent character that is qualitatively different from those of its component parts. Society is, therefore, not identical with the sum of individuals. It is, of course, true that without individuals there is no society. But society transcends the individual. While explaining social facts, it is important to understand the supremacy of the collective over the individual. He clarified,

> "The group thinks, feels, and acts quite differently from the way in which its members would were they isolated. If, then, we begin with the individual, we shall be able to understand nothing of what takes place in the group. In a word, there is between psychology and sociology the same break in continuity as between biology and the physiochemical sciences. Consequently every time that a social phenomenon is directly explained by a psychological phenomenon, we could be sure that the explanation is false" (1964: 104).

It was in this sense that Durkheim, as his other substantial works suggest, provided sociological explanations for social facts like suicide, division of labour and moral education. In fact, as Durkheim categorically stated, 'the determining cause of a social fact should be sought among the social facts preceding it and not among the states of individual consciousness.' In his opinion, the function of a social fact needs to be seen in its relation to some social end. He argued, 'to explain a social phenomenon is to find its cause as well as its function. And both cause and function are essentially social, not to be reduced to the individual psyche' (1964: 110).

The idealization of the natural sciences has become more pronounced during twentieth century, particularly, in the post-war era, major intellectual movements like behaviouralism, functionalism, structuralism, cognitivism, neopostivism, modernization theory continued to look to the natural sciences as their ideal for the study of human activity. The fact that Marx and Freud, and later theorists erred in their ambitions about developing their sciences into natural sciences is perhaps not so interesting today. But the general question of whether the natural science model is an appropriate ideal for the study of human activity remains timely. The question remains: must the "science of man" be different from natural science? (Flyvbjerg 2001: 27).

Debates over Methodology of Social Research

In social research, the debates over methodology were between those for whom social science is the explanation of social phenomena through a search for causes, that is, the social sciences methodologically is equivalent to the natural sciences, and those for whom social science is the understanding and interpretation of the meaning of social action. In other words, it involved not only the logical and epistemological issues of social science method, but also the ontological status of the objects of social science. It has a long history during which it has manifested itself in many forms.

In 1890s, in Germany, a dispute over methods in the field of economics was between Carl Menger (1841-1921), the neoclassical Austrian economist, and Gustan Schmoller (1838-1917) who belonged to the German younger economic history school. Menger insisted that the exact laws of theoretical economics were identical in form to those of the natural sciences such as mechanics. He was opposed by Schmoller who was also a member of the *Society for Social Policy* which was established in 1872 at Eisenach as a reform movement. The Society never took up concrete political programmes, instead it published several studies of specific concrete problems in the socio-economic sphere. For these studies, Schmoller advocated an inductive, empirical and historical approach in opposition to the deductive and abstract approach of Menger. When neo-Kantian philosophers entered the methodological debate, the dispute became generalized from a conflict over the methodology of economics to a conflict about methodology of social research.

Windelband (1848-1915) of the Heidelberg neo-Kantian school, distinguished the *nomothetic* natural sciences from the *ideographic* human sciences. For him, all explanations are of two types *nomothetic* and *ideographic*. The former refers to generalized laws and the latter to individual facts. In his view, this difference was not due to nature or society being the object of study of these sciences. But, the difference was the result of these sciences having distinct cognitive interests and goals. He pointed out that the natural sciences have a technical goal and interest while the human sciences have a practical goal and cognitive interest. Wilhem Dilthey (1833-1911) opposed Comte by posting a methodological divide between the natural sciences (*Naturwissenschaften)* and the human sciences (*Geisteswissenschaften)* which include social sciences. In his *Introduction to the Human Sciences*, he argued, "it was unfortunate that while the human sciences had successfully freed themselves from the domination of theology and metaphysics, they had succumbed to the domination of the natural sciences" (1883: 447). In fact, the dichotomy between the human science and the natural science was supposedly formalized by Dilthey in his distinction between Geisteswissenschaften and Naturwissenschaften, that is, between human sciences and natural sciences.

Another important conflict over the methodology of the social sciences, in Germany was the debate on the value and purpose of scientific research, which began in 1903 and lasted for over a decade, and in which a famous participant was Max Weber (1864-1920). Weber cut through the debate in his own particular way, although he numbered himself among the descendants of the historical school whose prominent thinkers were Schmoller and Windelband. For Weber, the social world was composed of unique objects and singular configurations. He did not reject causal analysis as inappropriate to the social sciences. Believing in the 'value relevance' of all social action, he saw the method of 'interpretative understanding' as essential to social science, but he also said that it had to be complemented by causal analysis. Not only did his category of 'value relevance' not exclude causal analysis, it also did not exclude his advocacy of a 'value-free' social science and this was the issue that he debated with Schmoller in the early 1900s (Weber 1949: 97).

On the question involving the ontological status of the objects of social sciences the dispute was between the individualists on one side and the holists on the other. It is, self-evidently, a philosophical question: when we speak of a social group, or a nation-state, or an economy, or a political system, what exactly do we mean? The best procedure is probably to follow the cyberneticists and to treat all collectivities as systems, such systems being operationally defined not as things but as sets of variables (Ashby 1956: 40). Explaining this, W.G. Runciman has put forward that for individualists, any statement about a collectivity must be in principle reducible to a set of statements about the individuals of whom the collectivity is composed. But the holists argue that in order to talk about – to give one of their favourite examples – a banking system we need to introduce concepts which depend for their meaning precisely on the fact that they can never be reduced to a list of assertions about individuals. Most of the disputants (apart, that is, from those who want to make extravagant statements about the 'group mind' or the 'organic state' or the 'collective unconscious') would probably agree that it is a mistake to speak of collectivities as having such things as ideas and purposes which can only be properly predicated of individual people (1969: 6). Max Weber is emphatic that what we are talking about when we say that a collectivity exists is a 'probability of action' appropriate in a specified way to the meaning attached to the collectivity. This does not mean that for some purposes (for instance, juristic) it may not be necessary to treat a business corporation or a state as if it were a person. It means that when a social researcher formulates a proposition about such a collectivity he must be able to specify the concrete social action which the proposition denotes. By this means, we can not only see how a given proposition might in principle, at least, be falsified, but we can also avoid treating a collectivity as if it were a tangible object – the 'fallacy of reification' which incenses the individualists (1969: 8).

On the question on the methodological equivalence, the dispute was between the positivists and the intuitionists. The positivists are those who in general regard the social sciences (under which they may well include history) as methodologically equivalent to the natural sciences; that is to say, they regard the differences between the two as being of a purely technical kind. Elaborating, Runciman put forward that the intuitionists strongly reject this claim, and they do so on one or both of two main grounds which need to be carefully distinguished. The first is that every historical event is unique in a way that the experiments or replications of natural science are not: an experiment can always be repeated, but never a segment of history. The second ground (which is, however, not entirely unrelated to the first) is that human behaviour has meaning to the agents performing it (1969: 8). To quote R. G. Collingwood, one of the most celebrated intuitionists, "Geology presents us with a series of events, but history is not history unless it presents us with a series of acts" (1946: 115).

According to the intutionists, the objects or events with which the natural scientist repeats his experiments or accumulates his examples can be treated as equivalent with each other. But no other person can be regarded as interchangeable: the events of which his action and intentions were a part, and which the historian wishes causally to explain, are wholly and intrinsically impossible to replicate. They argue that generalization is bound to be irrelevant: if the particular event has not been explained, it cannot be incorporated into a generalisation, whereas as if it has been explained, the generalization is unnecessary to explain it. Every historical event is unique and that this difference is an important one, we are not thereby driven defenceless into the intuitionist camp. For it is also true that all historical explanations depend at some point on the notion of 'what would have happened if...?', and this in turn does derive its validity from some general notions of cause. Without these, historians would be deprived of the use of even such words as 'dangerous'; and unless it is literally nonsense –which not even the most extreme intuitionists maintain – to assign proportional causal weights in any given (unique) historical sequence, then general explanations must have in principle some validity. Any explanation indeed, has implicit reference to a general law. No serious historian gives only a single reason in answer to the question why a particular event occurred. He gives instead a list of causes (or of necessary and sufficient conditions) whose relative importance it is his business to assign. His interpretation will depend on generalized or 'nomothetic' assumptions about historical cause and effect which could not possibly be solely deduced from the particular sequence he wishes to explain. It therefore follows, Runciman writes, that both intuitionists and positivists are partly right, but neither is altogether as right as they have been apt to claim. Every historical sequence is unique, but this does not deny validity to general causal explanations. General causal explanations have validity but, history is not reducible entirely to determinate instances of fully articulated sets of such laws. The historian (and therefore the social scientist) can never be a thoroughgoing positivist but, he must, once he has realized this, still try to behave up to a point as though he were (1969: 10).

According to Runciman, the second major intuitionist argument, which derives from the assertion that human behaviour is (unlike that of the objects of natural science) meaningful, raises some of the most far-reaching philosophical issues of all. But without entering into the logical complexities of motives and intentions, we may initially follow Weber in regarding social behaviour as meaningful by definition. For Weber, 'action' covers all behaviour to which a subjective meaning is attached by the agent, and social action covers all action which takes account of the behaviour of others by virtue of the subjective meaning attached to it by the agent. This excludes, for instance, lunacy of certain kinds. But although such behaviour may require explanation just as much as any other, the social scientist is not as such concerned with it once it ceases to fulfil Weber's definition. The crucial question is how far the meaningfulness of social action makes a social science impossible (1969: 11).

It would obviously be absurd to claim to have explained, Runciman elaborates, a sequence of social behaviour without having any idea of what it means to the participants. This will apply, moreover, even if our observation of successive uniformities enables us to make verified predictions about the course of this behaviour. If, for example, an observer watches a group of people who under certain circumstances exchange small pieces of paper and metal, after which one of them gives another an object which the recipient then takes away, he may in due course be able to make accurate predictions about the transfer of goods in this community by correlating such transfers with the exchange of metal pieces. But unless he has grasped the ideas of money, buying and selling, and so on, we shall deny his claim to have explained what is going on. This sort of illustration appears at first sight to force us back among the intuitionists again; and indeed, some interpreters of Weber have taken his sense of *Verstehen* to entail an intuitionist position. But this is not so. Weber is emphatic that even the most self-evident interpretation requires to be validated – Weber, indeed, is prepared to use the word 'verified' – by reference to concrete empirical evidence (1969: 12). For Weber, "verification of subjective interpretation by comparison with the concrete course of events is, as in the case of all hypotheses, indispensable" (1949: 97).

Finally, there was the post Second World War debate on positivism or positivist dispute in Germany, which began in 1961 with Karl Popper's opening address to the German Sociological Association at Tubingen. Popper presented twenty-seven theses on the logic of the social sciences, and Adorno answered him. The debate was between a supposedly positivist methodology advocated by Popper and Adorno's anti-positivist stance, but Popper spiked the proceedings somewhat claiming himself to be critic of positivism. Few scholars considered that Popper's affiliation was not quite to either of the schools which can be broadly labelled intuitionists and positivists. Popper is not only opposed to intuitionism, which he wishes to assimilate by force to the hypothetical method of natural science; he is also opposed to positivism, in that his fiercest onslaughts are directed against any attempt to construct a predictive science of history. This is not as inconsistent as it might appear, for his objection to what he calls 'historicism' is on technical grounds which need not always conflict with his wish to equate the 'understanding' involved in both natural and social science. Moreover, much of his objection to 'historicism' derives from his position on the individualist/holistic dispute, for

Popper is the founding father of the so-called 'methodological individualists' (Runciman, 1969: 14). In spite of this, the dispute continued with Habermas (1929-) coming in on the side of Adorno (1903-1969) and continuing the attack on Popper's methodology as positivist, and Hans Albert (1904-1973) defending this methodology. In this debate too, as in the earlier ones, one side insisted on the human/historical/cultural/social sciences having their own methodology, distinct from that of natural science. The name given to this distinct methodology of the human sciences was hermeneutics.

Karl Popper (1902-1994), a leading philosopher of science in the twentieth century, came forward with his distinctive idea of science which changed our understanding of science and society. He was profoundly influenced by the changes in physics that emerged out of Einstein's theory of relativity which revealed that Newtonian physics, which was dominant for more than two hundred years, could be interrogated. This led him to plead for the relative character of science. Science is not something solid and stable, or eternally valid. Instead, science, for him, is a set of conjectures subject to falsification and refutation. In *Conjectures and Refutation: the Growth of Scientific Knowledge*, Popper asserted, "No wonder the creation of the scientific status of a theory is its falsifiability, or refutability or testability" (1972: 37). A theory which is not refutable by any conceivable event, he reminded us, is non-scientific. Contrary to popular belief, irrefutability is not a virtue of science. The challenge confronting the scientific community is not to search for confirmations/verifications of the existing theory, but to search for falsification and refutation. It is not at all necessary to absolutise or sanctify any particular source of knowledge, be it Baconian empiricism or Cartesian rationality, and think that the knowledge gained through it is a domain of absolute certainty. This would lead to dogmatic thinking and generate a false belief that the world is full of verifications of the existing theory. He critiqued this dogmatic thinking, and argued that science could progress only through an open culture promoting the spirit of refutability and falsifiability (1972: 27). It is only through this culture of "critical rationalism" that science progresses. Science is inherently critical and democratic, perpetually progressing through trial and error, conjectures and refutations. But pseudo-science is dogmatic; it is too certain of its explanatory power, it sees only confirmations and verifications. In other words, Popper gave a new meaning to science, and sought to free science from positivistic certainties. Science, for him, is relative; science is like myth-making. And what promotes science is not the arrogance emanating from cognitive certainty, but a spirit of humbleness that encourages the possibility of falsifiability and refutability (1972: 35).

Weber does get some mild credit from Popper for seeing that intuitive understanding must always be controlled by ordinary scientific canons and methods (Popper 1957: 292). But at the same time criticizing Weber for being an intuitionist, he disregards Weber's essential point. He opined that 'despite the need for scientific controls wherever possible, the meaningful nature of social behaviour requires that it should be explained in terms additional to those adequate for the natural sciences' (Popper 1961: 145). The point is rather that 'science in Popper's sense of science is not by itself an adequate description of their goal' (Runciman 1969: 14).

Thomas Kuhn (1922-1996) was yet another major philosopher of science who apprised us about normal science and it inherent conservatism, and extraordinary science leading to scientific revolutions. In *The Structure of Scientific Revolution,* he wrote,

> "Normal science consists in the actualization of that promise, an actualization achieved by extending the knowledge of those facts that the paradigm displays as particularly revealing, by increasing the extent of the match between those facts and the paradigm's predictions, and by further articulation of the paradigm itself" (1970: 23).

For him, normal science relies on the centrality of the paradigm that a particular scientific community takes for granted. According to him, 'paradigms are some accepted examples of actual scientific practice, examples which include law, theory, application, and instrumentation together, that provide models from which arise particular coherent traditions of scientific research' (1970: 10). A paradigm, in other words, provides the background, and directs the trajectory of normal science. Its power lies in its ability to attract an enduring group of adherents away from competing modes of scientific activity. It was in this sense that Newton's Principia and Optics, Franklin's Electricity and Einstein's Theory of Relativity acted as paradigms at different junctures of scientific history. He opined that normal science does not seek to refute, falsify or interrogate the prevalent paradigm. Instead, it seeks to actualize the potential of the paradigm itself, and resolve all residual ambiguities through further elaboration, experimentation and fact-gathering activities. And, paradoxically, it is this conservatism that leads to the cumulative progress of normal science. But then, there are situations when the crisis/anomaly begin to confront the scientific community. It may arise because of the persistent failure of normal science to make sense of the new phenomenon. This crisis situation leads to extraordinary science. It is extraordinary because, unlike normal science, it acknowledges the crisis, interrogates the established paradigm, and dares to become innovative (1970: 90). And eventually, it is this extraordinary science that leads to a 'paradigm shift' resulting in scientific revolutions. It was the way Einstein, to take a specific example, made a revolution in physics. The revolutionary or new paradigm is incompatible with the earlier one.

Indeed, Kuhn repeatedly emphasized on the 'incommensurability of paradigms'. For him, periods with scientific revolutions are a consequence of periods with stable, normal-science research, in that it is via the daily normal "puzzle solving" that the anomalies and contradictions appear which gradually undermine the original paradigm. The resulting crisis continues until the anomalies and contradictions can be explained within a new paradigm; that is, until researchers experience "the pieces suddenly sorting themselves out and coming together in a new way" (1987: 9). The result is a new paradigm around which there is again general agreement and on the basis of which normal-science research can again be conducted. According to him, it is not easy for the scientific community to accept the new paradigm, because massive conservatism/dogmatism characterize the community of normal scientists. It is, however, important to realise that, despite this resistance, the new paradigm succeeds in attracting more and more adherents, and eventually establishes its hegemony. The new paradigm appeals because it is said to be 'neater', 'more suitable', or 'simpler' than the old (1970: 91).

Thus, in Kuhn's view natural sciences are relatively cumulative. His famous phenomenological evolutionary scheme for the natural sciences contains long periods with stable normal science; that is, periods with a generally accepted mode of conducting research. The researcher's work in such periods consists in what he calls "puzzle solving" within the framework of a common, accepted "paradigm." The stable periods of normal science are at times broken by periods of radical instability and "revolutionary" change. After a time, change leads to a new paradigm, to cumulative replacement in which the old paradigm becomes superfluous (Flyvbjerg 2001: 27).

Kuhn's now-classic description of the research process was criticized for introducing an element of relativism within the natural sciences and in the theory and history of science, a critique which has recently been restated by physicist Steven Weinberg (1998: 48-52). Kuhn apparently activated the Cartesian anxiety of natural scientists, and of philosophers and historians of science. A similar critique and anxiety has been directed at Foucault, Derrida, and other non essentialist thinkers. The matter is far from settled, but it is clear for most observers, that even though natural-science theory, following Kuhn, cannot be seen as entirely so constant and cumulative as previously assumed, there is still room for a degree of stability and progress for these sciences. Therefore the ambition has continued to be to emulate the natural-science model in the study of human affairs, especially as regards the development of theory which is typically seen as the pinnacle of scientific endeavour.

Social Science Methodology: Distinct From Natural-Science Model

Since Kuhn's *The Structure of Scientific Revolutions*, natural science has been further relativized via what could be called the "universality of hermeneutics," argued by scholars as diverse as Paul Feyerabend (1924-1994), Richard Rorty (1931-2007), Harold Garfinkel (1917-2011), Hans-Georg Gadamer (1900-2002), Jurgen Habermas (1929-), Paul Ricoeur (1913-2005), Michel Foucault (1926-1984), Anthony Giddens (1938-) and, since the late 1970s by Kuhn himself. To quote Kuhn, "what I as a physicist had to discover for myself, most historians learn by example in the course of professional training. Consciously or not, they are all practitioners of the hermeneutic method" (1977: xiii).

Paul Feyerabend (1924-1994) who critiqued the hegemony of scientific method, was of the opinion that 'no method, even the most successful one, has the right to subdue and marginalize other methods.' In *Science in a Free* Society, published in 1982, he refused to give his consent to scientism, that is, the belief that science is the only valid form of knowledge. Instead, he revealed the politics of science, its relationship with power, and the way through propaganda and other strategies it murdered all alternative forms of knowledge. He insisted that scientism would go against the true spirit of a democratic society, because democracy should imply the plurality of knowledge systems, methods and traditions of enquiry. He opined that 'each tradition, each fairy tale, each story, has its validity.' He believed, 'nothing is dead or meaningless.' It is important that we embrace an 'anarchist theory of knowledge' implying that everything is possible' (1982).

Richard Rorty (1931-2007) put forward, there is a fundamental distinction between normal and non-normal science, a distinction which cuts across the boundary separating the study of human affairs on the one hand and the study of nature on the other. In *Philosophy and the Mirror of Nature*, he wrote;

> "The line . . . is not the line between the human and the nonhuman but between that portion of the field of inquiry where we feel rather uncertain that we have the right vocabulary at hand and that portion where we feel rather certain that we do. This does, at the moment, roughly coincide with the distinction between the fields of the *Geistes-* and the *Naturwissenschaften* but this coincidence may be mere coincidence" (1979: 352).

Hans-Georg Gadamer (1900-2002) took the discussion on methodology in social science research to a different plane. In *Truth and Method* (1985) he argued that if one were to take seriously the claim of understanding being a category of life, then one could not see hermeneutics narrowly as a methodological tool, but one had to instead speak of "universal" hermeneutics, since all human experience has a hermeneutic dimension. He categorically stated that the hermeneutics he was developing was not a methodology of the human sciences. He raised philosophical questions: "what is understanding, and how is understanding possible?" He defined hermeneutics as the "basic being-in-motion of There-being which constitutes its finiteness and historicity and hence includes the whole of its experience of the world." The study of hermeneutics is thus the study of Being and ultimately, the study of language, because "Being that can be understood is language" (as quoted in Hekman 1986: 94). According to him, in an unselfconscious manner, we are engaged in the hermeneutic task of understanding all the time, but we only become conscious of it when we have an experience of misunderstanding, when we feel that we have not read the situation correctly. Just as breathing is a constant part of us as long as we live, so is understanding a part of our being in the world.

Explaining his concept of 'explanatory understanding,' Jurgen Habermas (1929-) said,

> "The What, the meaningful content of the systematically distorted expression, cannot be "understood" if the Why, the origin of the symptomatic scene in the conditions responsible for the systematic distortion itself, cannot be "explained" at the same time... explanatory understanding, as a depth-hermeneutical deciphering of specifically inaccessible expressions, presupposes not only, as simple hermeneutical understanding does, the trained application of naturally acquired communicative competence, but a theory of communicative competence as well. Such a theory concerns itself with the forms of the inter-subjectivity of language and the causes of their deformation" (1985: 305).

He argues that the methodological structure of Freudian psychoanalysis is paradigmatic for a critical science of society. He calls the method of psychoanalysis a form of 'depth hermeneutics'; which incorporates explanation and understanding into a science oriented towards 'methodological self-reflection.' According to him, 'successful psychoanalytic practice is defined in terms of the patient himself or herself being able to understand and overcome his or her neurosis' (Ibid.). This idea can be generalized to the position that human beings, unlike objects in nature, have a consciousness and an understanding of what it is that they are doing. If the social scientist does not want to stay limited to this understanding, she or he is also not to ignore it by calling it false consciousness.

In his *The Model of the Text* (1971), Paul Ricoeur (1913-2005), in order to justify the relevance of hermeneutics as a method to the social sciences, put forward that human actions have the same structure as a written text. He distinguishes between spoken and written discourse. In written discourse, unlike in an oral conversation, the link between the author and the meaning of what the author has written, as well as the link between the meaning of what is written and the specific interlocutor to whom it is addressed, is broken. According to him, the objective meaning of a text is something other than the subjective intention of the author, and so the problem of the right understanding can no longer be solved by a simple return to the alleged intention of the author. Not that hermeneutics, even in the hands of Schleiermacher and Dilthey, ever reduced meaning to intentionality, but what is new in Ricoeur is that he begins to speak of the transition 'from Understanding to Explanation' and 'from Explanation to Understanding.'

The hermeneutic-phenomenological argument takes its point of departure in a critical difference between natural and social sciences: the former studies physical objects while the latter studies self-reflecting humans and must therefore take account of changes in the interpretations of the objects of study. Stated in another way, 'in social science, the object is a subject' (Flyvbjerg 2001: 32). According to Anthony Giddens, "the technical language and theoretical propositions of the natural sciences are insulated from the world with which they are concerned because that world does not answer back. But social theory cannot be insulated from its "object-world," which is a subject-world" (1982: 13). He put forward the concept of "double hermeneutics". First are the self-interpretations among those people the researchers study. For Giddens, these self-interpretations and their relations to the context of those studied must be understood in order to understand why people act as they do. The second aspect of the double hermeneutic concerns the researchers' own self-interpretations. Just as the people studied are part of a context, research itself also constitutes a context, and the researchers are a part of it. The researchers' self-understanding and concepts do not exist in a vacuum, but must be understood in relation to this context. He stated, "Context both determines and is determined by the researchers' self-understanding" (1982: 7).

The ethnomethodology of Harold Garfinkel gave emphasis to the second part of the double hermeneutic. He pointed out that the basic skills which researchers in the social sciences must possess in order to carry out their work are just as situational, just as dependent on the context, as the interpretations of the people whom the researchers study. People's daily activities, regardless of how trivial they may seem, and the researchers' work within the sciences, are both objects of the ethnomethodologists' scrutiny (Flyvbjerg 2001: 33). Describing the field of ethnomethodological inquiry, he stated, "no inquiries can be excluded no matter where or when they occur, no matter how vast or trivial their scope" (1984: 32).

In *The Order of Things,* Michel Foucault postulated that the study of individuals and society, what he calls the "human sciences," understands human beings in a dual manner, as both constituting what counts as facts in these sciences and at the same time as an object for theoretical and empirical research. He turns the perspective from the self-interpretation in the double hermeneutic of those being studied and the researchers doing the studying to humankind's double role as both meaning giver (subjects, who give things meaning by deciding what counts as an object) and as the "meaningless" objects of study, whom the subjects study and on whom meaning is rendered (1973: 344). He opined, 'if one wishes to understand human knowing, it is necessary to understand both poles of this duality.' According to him, however, this attempt to understand what makes understanding possible drives the study of human activity into an "essential instability" (1973: 364).

Whereas hermeneutics according to Wilhelm Dilthey and, in part, to Max Weber was regarded as an activity linked only to the study of human activity, it is now argued that the natural sciences are also historically conditioned and require hermeneutic interpretation. In other words, the natural science ideal cannot even be found in the natural sciences themselves. Natural scientists, too, must determine what constitutes relevant facts, methods, and theories; for example, what would count as "nature." These determinations are made on the basis of a common interpretation of what constitutes scientific work. Interpretation tends to occur implicitly, but is, nevertheless, interpretation which "is acquired as tacit practical skills and conventions via training in the actual performance of scientific activity" (Flyvbjerg 2001: 28).

Methodological Position of Social Research: The Present State

It is evident from the debate on the methodology of social research that there were several variants of it. From evolutionary perspective, it began with the idolization of the natural–science model as an ideal type for social science research. Later on, this assumption was negated by theorists who believed in the relative character of natural science and in their opinion, the natural science itself can be interrogated. They argued that the natural-science ideal cannot even be found in the natural sciences. In some interpretations, this development runs counter to the assumption that science will eventually describe nature's universal laws. Complexity, chance, irreversibility, time, and evolution have made their entry into physics and have led to debates as to whether this prototype of natural science can be epistemic in the classical Aristotelian sense. Convergence between the natural and social sciences on the basis of seeing both as dealing with complex systems has been argued by the Gulbekian Commission on the Restructuring of the Social Sciences (Mudimbe 1996: 78-9). Following this view, some have thought that a unified social and natural science is possible, analogous to the argument of the universality of hermeneutics, because natural sciences reveal themselves to have the same non-epistemic status as social sciences, and not because the social sciences can become epistemic like the natural sciences. We may agree with this argument insofar as the natural sciences' foundation now seems epistemologically more complex than previously thought. But the existence of an identity between social and natural sciences on one point does not necessarily mean that they are the same. One cannot overlook the difference in results between the natural and the social sciences. Epistemic vocabularies have worked successfully in relation to their own intentions within particular domains in the natural sciences with no parallel in the social sciences. However, the fact that the epistemic vocabularies have worked effectively in some areas does not necessarily mean that such vocabularies are universal, or that the Great Book of Nature can be written in the language of mathematics, as Galileo asserted. Neither argument is sufficient for making the case of a possible unified thinking of the natural and the social sciences (Flyvbjerg 2001: 29-30).

The social sciences do not evolve via scientific revolutions, as Kuhn says is the case for the natural sciences. Rather, as pointed out by Hubert Dreyfus, social sciences go through periods where various constellations of power and waves of intellectual fashion dominate, and where a change from one period to another, which on the surface may resemble a paradigm shift, actually consists of the researchers within a given area abandoning a "dying" wave for a growing one, without having occurred any collective accumulation of knowledge. Not paradigm shifts but rather style changes are what characterize social science: it is not a case of evolution but more of fashion. Foucault poses the question of whether it is reasonable at all to use the label "science" for this kind of activity. Even the expression "body of knowledge" is too pretentious for Foucault: "let us say, to be more neutral still . . . body of discourse." The social sciences have always found themselves in a situation of constant reorganization, characterized by a multiplicity of directions. It is not a state of crisis in a Kuhnian sense, that is, of a period with competing paradigms located between periods with normal science. The condition of the social sciences has been termed "pre-paradigmatic," if we remain in the Kuhnian terminology. The social sciences have always been in this state and as a result are neither relatively cumulative nor relatively stable.

To maintain that the study of human and society finds itself in a pre-paradigmatic stage is to imply that a coming "maturation" of the social sciences will produce a more desirable paradigmatic stage characterized by normal science. It is argued that the study of human society is somewhat younger than the natural sciences; the social sciences have not benefited from the same resources as has the study of nature; their object of study – human activity – is more complex; their conceptual apparatus and research methods need to be more refined; and with more time for further development and refinement, there should, in principle, be nothing in the way of the social sciences achieving the same paradigmatic stage as the natural sciences, becoming cumulative, stable, and predictive. This is the essence of what is here called the "pre-paradigmatic argument."

According to the pre-paradigmatic argument, both the natural and the social sciences may find themselves in periods where they are cumulative, stable, and predictive, and both may also experience periods with confusing and incorrect predictions. The immature state of social science on which this argument is based has nothing to do with fundamental properties of human beings or of social science. For example, even though political scientists may disagree as to what constitutes "the political," while physicists seem to be in more agreement as to what constitute physical phenomena, this state of affairs does not necessarily have to remain permanent. According to the pre-paradigmatic argument, there is nothing in principle which prevents political scientists from being able to reach agreement concerning the political domain, nor physicists from again disagreeing as to the basic categories of nature, as they did when quantum theory first appeared.

The pre-paradigmatic argument is lucrative. First because it entails a high degree of methodological clarity for the study of human activity, where, following the argument, it models itself on the well-developed and well-tested methodology of the natural sciences for theory development. Second, the natural sciences have had inordinately great success with their methodology. Could the social sciences achieve similar results if they developed their research methods sufficiently far along the natural science path? Yes, the argument goes. It is therefore not surprising that the pre-paradigmatic argument is popular among many social scientists. The argument tends to constitute the conventional wisdom within positivist and neopositivist thinking in the social sciences and it is also a key element in various types of functionalism (Flyvbjerg 2001: 30-32).

Belief in the pre-paradigmatic argument provides the basis for a good portion of optimism within social science. But the fact remains that today's natural-science-modelled social sciences are no more "normal" and have no more predictive success than their seemingly less sophisticated predecessors. After more than three hundred years of attempts, one could reasonably expect that there would exist at least a sign that social science has moved in the desired direction, that is, toward predictive theory. It has not. And when the social sciences are compared with relatively new natural sciences such as meteorology and biology, which also struggle with especially complicated objects of study, it can be seen that the latter exhibit slow, but relatively cumulative, progress. These relatively new natural sciences have evolved ever more complex theories which account for an increasing range of phenomena, while social science typically seeks to develop theories pertaining to one class of phenomena and then abandons these for theories which include another. The social sciences appear unable to demonstrate the kind of progress which is supposed to characterize normal science.

2

Growth of Social Research

Social science research or, to put it more specifically, social research, as a formal body of knowledge that has grown, evolved, created a community of scholars, and established as a distinctive tradition of the study of human activity. In the course of its growth and development, it has established for itself a method, a set of principles or guidelines for observing the social reality, and constructing a systematic body of knowledge. In other words, it is a formal, structured body of knowledge having its own technical idioms and vocabulary, and distinctive ways of collecting data and arriving at generalisations. Social scientists, it is argued, are "objective" and "value-neutral"; they rely on hard empirical facts, and the social science account is, therefore, not an ideological, subjective, valorisations or condemnation of social reality. It is often believed that understanding methodology of social research is like comprehending the very philosophy of modern science that gave an identity to social science.

The philosophic roots of modern science can be traced back to the seventeenth century thinkers Francis Bacon (1561-1626) and Rene Descartes (1564-1650). If Francis Bacon provided the foundations of empiricism or what is known as the method of induction, Rene Descartes taught us the fundamental lessons of rationalism or deductive reasoning. Bacon taught us the first important lesson of objectivity: how to spell out the book of nature as it is, and, how to observe it without any pre-selection and bias. For Bacon, there are many delusions that act as obstacles and divert us from truth. As a result, we confuse the reality with our own subjective idea of it. A knower must overcome all these delusions that Bacon regarded as the 'idols of mind'. He postulated that there are four species of idols that: *idols of the tribe, idols of the den, idols of the market,* and, *idols of the theatre.* For Bacon, these idols are essentially obstacles and must be overcome. Only then is it possible to see and observe the world without bias. For him, "human minds are like 'uneven mirrors' that distort the reality" (1970: 92). In other words, nature exists out there, and it is only pure empiricism, not contaminated by our feelings and sentiments, that can grasp it. And this objective knowledge, he believed, would enable human beings to establish their superiority over nature. It is in this sense that knowledge is indeed power. And the relationship between the knower and the known is detached and impersonal; the vulnerability of the self of the knower is controlled, and the act of knowing becomes a dispassionate exercise. On the other hand, Descartes argued, it was through pure rationality that human beings could arrive at truth and became free from all uncertainties and errors. For him, the sense could not be reliable source of knowledge; the senses could deceive one. As a result in an act of meditation, he began to doubt everything that he learned through the sense. Yet there was one thing Descartes felt certain about. Even if a demon deceived him, the fact that he was being deceived confirmed his existence as a thinking being. In other words, as he argued, 'man is a thing that thinks.' This led him to privilege the indivisible mind that makes one think, and separate it from the non-thinking body. For him, while one cannot separate oneself from one's mind, one can, however, exist without one's body! (1641: 467). Through his concept of mind/body dualism he conveyed, what provides solid foundations is a distinctively rational thought emanating from the indivisible, integrated, coherent mind. And this rational thought is pure, abstract, disembodied, completely dissociated from the senses, from pain and pleasure, from feelings and emotions. Thus, these two fundamentals, namely, objective empiricism of Bacon, and disembodied rationality of Descartes provided the methodological basis to the study of nature, and human activity.

Like all great movements which transform an entire society, science drew its strength from a combination of factors. By the seventeenth century most of these factors had come into play and begun to reinforce one another. The "natural philosopher" who laid the foundations of modern science coupled theory with practice; tested their theories by the experimental method; used mathematics, the "language of number", whenever possible to express the laws they discerned; and shared their knowledge and their discoveries with their fellow scientists. All these procedures had been utilized to some extent in earlier times and in other societies. But never before had students of the physical world pursued all four procedures simultaneously with such enthusiasm and insight as the Europeans were displaying by the seventeenth century. The result was a rapid increase in scientific knowledge, a flood of discoveries and inventions sometimes called "scientific revolution of the seventeenth century" (Ferguson 1958: 575).

Leonardo da Vinci (1452-1519) observed early in the sixteenth century, "Science is the captain, practice the soldiers." A hundred years later Galileo (1564-1642) declared that those who liked to theorize about nature ought to go into the shops and shipyards and watch artisans and mechanics at work. Francis Bacon (1561-1626), in his *Novum Organum* (1620), warned that "neither the hand without instruments, nor the unassisted understanding, can do much." But he insisted that great progress would result from a combination of theory and practice, or as he phrased it, "from the close and strict union of the experimental and rational faculties, which have not hitherto been united." Galileo proclaimed, "True philosophy expounds nature to us; but she can be understood only by him who has learned the speech and symbols in which she speaks to us. This speech is mathematics, and its symbols are mathematical figures." To Descartes the physical universe appeared to be a vast machine created by a supreme mathematician. He declared, "The laws of nature are identical with the laws of mechanics. You can substitute 'the mathematical order of the universe' for 'God' whenever I use the latter term." It remained for the greatest mathematician of the age, Isaac Newton (1642-1727) to reduce these inferences to order and explain the movements of all bodies, earthly and celestial, as expressions of one general principle. He reached his epoch-making conclusion in 1665 at the age of twenty-three, but he did not publish it until 1687. Then, in his immortal *Principia*, he offered mathematical proofs for his hypothesis that the force of attraction between two bodies varies directly as the product of their masses and inversely as the square of the distance between them. To test this principle he applied it to explain the movements of the moon about the earth, and when he found his figures working out correctly, he was so deeply stirred by his discovery that he had to ask a friend to finish the calculations for him. As a further verification he extended his computations to the planets, to the tides, even to the apparent vagaries of visiting comets, and found that all. For this, he praised the contribution of earlier philosophers, "if I have seen farther than Descartes, it is by standing on the shoulders of giants." What occurred in the seventeenth century was the sudden acceleration of a process which had been long in the making and which was to increase its momentum, in the centuries that followed, with ever more astonishing results (Ferguson 1958: 576-79). Thus, the successes won by the scientific method in the seventeenth century fostered the growth of a more secular and rationalistic spirit in European society and helped to make the eighteenth century an "Age of Reason."

In the eighteenth century, the Enlightenment, an intellectual movement, primarily in France and Britain, that spans approximately one hundred years from the 1680s to 1789 was really a turning point, a breakthrough that generated a new way of seeing, and celebrated the science of Bacon, Descartes and Newton as the most cherished and legitimate body of knowledge. The leading representatives of Enlightenment were Hobbes (1588-1679), Locke (1632-1704), Voltaire (1694-1778), Montesquieu (1689-1755), Francois Quesnay (1694-1774), Rousseau (1712-1778), Denis Diderot (1713-1784), Adam Smith (1723-1790), Marquis Beccaria (1738-1794), and Immanuel Kant (1724-1804). They were religious sceptics, political reformers, cultural critics, historians and social theorists.

Liberal thinkers everywhere urged that manners, morals and modes of government, religion and education should be analysed rationally, brought to perfection or discard. Once the existing laws and institutions had been perfected, the rationalists felt confident that humanity would undergo a miraculous regeneration. They imagined that the millennium was at hand because they had found a fruitful method for investigating the world about them, and they leaped to the false conclusion that this method could be applied to the social sciences with the same success. Some ages ask questions, others answer them. The eighteenth century was of the latter type. Its intellectual leaders hoped to find the answers to all the problems of society; they burned to apply them, and infected all classes with their contagious enthusiasm. It is not difficult to understand why the century was loud with projects of reform, nor surprising that it should have ended with a revolution.

In contrast to systems of thought where the sacred had dominated and where questioning was discouraged, the Enlightenment thinkers viewed human reason as dominant. No subjects of study were to be forbidden, there were no unaskable questions, with all aspects of human life appropriate for examination and study. In doing this, they combined the philosophic tradition of abstract rational thought of Descartes and other philosophers with the tradition of experimentation or empirical philosophy from Galilei, Newton, Bacon and others. The result was a new system of human inquiry that attacked the old order and privileges, put emphasis and faith on science, the scientific method and education, and acquired and practical function of asking critical questions about existing institutions and demanding that the unreasonable ones, those contrary to human nature, be changed. All social obstacles to human perfectibility were to be progressively eliminated (Zeitlin 1990: 2).

SOCIO-ECONOMIC CONDITIONS IN EUROPE BEFORE THE FRENCH REVOLUTION

With the Intellectual Revolution a spirit of rationalism and scepticism had spread among the enlightened classes of society. In France the movement was particularly strong which was led by a unique group of writers who are known as the *philosophes* or philosophers. No tradition or institution was sacred to these critics, who delighted in holding up to public ridicule the stupidly, hypocrisy, and irrationality of existing customs, and who pleaded, in the name of humanity and right reason, for a programme of intelligent reforms. The philosophers were against the prevailing system of government and the organization of society under which the European people lived before the French Revolution (1789). It was an outmoded and inefficient system with glaring deficiencies. "The wreckage of feudalism still weighed like an incubus upon society, and governments functioned in a makeshift and haphazard fashion" (Ferguson 1958:586). They highlighted the defects and abuses of the prevailing socio-economic conditions which incited the French people to rise against the system.

Similar conditions existed with local variations throughout most of Europe. In almost all the European states, monarchs had made their authority supreme, the divine-right monarchy was established in theory and practice. "The will of the king was law." The king held his office through hereditary right, an office glorified by tradition and sanctified by religion. But, in practice, the royal government was dependent upon a host of subordinate officials who supplied him with information and exercised delegated powers in his name.

In France, under Louis XV (1715-74), it was governed in reality by the ministers of the royal council. These councillors sometimes met together with the king presiding, but more often assembled in smaller committees, as the council of state, commerce, and council of war. As the functions of the councils were not very clearly defined, there was much confusion, and business piled up more rapidly than it could be dispatched. Confusion in the capital bred chaos in the provinces. The power of royal official known as the *intendant* had grown so great that they were called in the eighteenth century the "thirty tyrants" of France. The centralization of authority in the hands of the bureaucracy had stifled the initiative and enterprise of local officials, who found it easiest to refer every difficult decision to their superiors. The royal government of France was no worse than that of Spain or Austria; it was served by many hard-working and intelligent administrators; but their efforts were of little avail in a system which seemed to have been specially devised to perpetuate confusion and procrastination. What the state required was a radical and exhaustive reconstruction in every branch of the administration. The partial and often capricious reforms instituted by the ministers in the hope of clearing a way through the disorder only added to the confusion. Their instructions were commonly so involved, so lengthy, and so loaded with amendments that their subordinates found it impossible to master them. Critics of the old regime in every state in Europe were agreed that the reform of paramount importance was the preparation of a simple and unified code of laws. An absolute Monarch, it was urged, might bring order out of the existing chaos by defining the duties and functions of his government in a few logical and invariable rules. Or, if the prince neglected his duty, the people themselves might prepare a constitution which would safeguard their liberties by establishing the government on true and inflexible principles. Throughout society, from the king's councillors to the petty tradesmen in provincial towns, irritation at the administrative disorder was growing into a passion (Ferguson 1958: 586-7).

Social Stratification

The feudal stratification of society into three classes, clergy, nobility and commoners ('Third Estate'), become unjust and illogical by the eighteenth century. In France, a country with perhaps twenty-five million people, the clergy and nobility constituted less than two per cent of the population, yet they enjoy the income from the richest lands of the kingdom, were exempted from the most onerous taxes, and occupied by right of rank the highest and best paid offices in the government, the army, and the church. The Roman Catholic Church in France owned approximately one-fifth of the land. The Church itself paid no taxes to the king on its property, but the clergy voted "free gifts" to the royal exchequer from time to time as a scanty substitute. Part of the revenue of the Church went for charitable purpose, part as salary for the 130,000 clergy; but the salaries were very unevenly distributed. Many abbots and bishops, nobles by birth in most cases, disposed of princely incomes, but the humble and hardworking parish priests were often no better off than the peasants among whom they laboured. This impending revolution was to prove that many village *cures* had less loyalty to the First Estate to which they nominally belonged than to the Third Estate whose grievances they understood. The second privileged class, the nobles, numbered about 110,000 souls, and likewise enjoyed the income from about one-fifth of the land. As a rule this land was cultivated by tenants who paid the noble owner rent and services for the privilege. Some of the nobles did not even reside on their estates, preferring the more amusing and expensive life at court. Bailiffs collected from the tenants the income which these absentee landlords often squandered on gambling and display. There was a further injustice in the fact that the nobles who enjoyed this unearned revenue, amassed by the toil of others, were free from the more burdensome taxes which the impoverished peasant had to pay. The millions of unprivileged subjects who made up the Third Estate had grievances that were concrete and specific. The heavy and unequal taxes were a special source of bitterness. All the ranks of the unprivileged, the upper middle class, the lower middle class, the artisans, the servants, the peasants, down to the thieves and vagabonds of the highway, hated the fiscal system. This was not surprising since the burden of taxation rested most heavily upon those least able to support it and crushed the peasant most cruelly of all. For in addition to the rent and services paid to the lord of the manor, and the tithe paid to the church, poor peasants had to discharge a land tax (the *taille*), a poll tax, an income tax, and a salt tax (the *gabelle*). Peasants too poor to buy food were still compelled to purchase salt at exorbitant prices, and if they attempted to smuggle enough for their need in order to avoid paying the royal revenue on it, they were punished with barbarous severity.

The middle-class dwellers in the towns though better off than the peasants, were even more critical and discontented. The professional and business classes, the bourgeoisie, included the most cultured, the most intelligent, and the most progressive elements in the nation. From the bourgeois class came the most competent officials in the king's service; it included the bankers who tided the government over its financial crises with their loans, and the businessmen who increased the prosperity of the state by their commercial and industrial enterprise. Yet this energetic and intelligent class was denied political power, and its members were forced to accept a position of inferiority, while the higher offices in the church, the army, the law courts, and the diplomatic service were bestowed upon men whose only claim to preference was their noble birth. Knowing their own worth and importance, conscious that in wealth, ability and education they were the equals of the titled few, ambitious members of the bourgeoisie hated the system which denied them their deserts. They possessed both the intelligence and the motive for starting revolution, and they fed their discontent by studying the abuses in the government, particularly those connected with the administration of law and the collection of taxes (Ibid.: 588-90).

Administration

The confusion of authority under the old regime is well illustrated by the condition of the law courts. Instead of a uniform code of laws in force throughout the nation, France possessed some three hundred and sixty differing codes, with the inevitable result that jurisdictions overlapped, decisions conflicted, and cases multiplied. Moreover, an offense punishable in one court by a fine might earn branding or ten years in the galleys from another, although it was obvious, as the rationalists pointed out, that there could not be several penalties for the same crime and all of them just. The humane spirit of the age was further shocked by the barbarous practices of judicial torture, mutilation, branding, and breaking on the wheel. But the worst terror in this legal jungle was the arbitrary power of the king and his ministers, who could imprison any citizen without warning, without trial, and without appeal, and on the sole authority of a royal *letter de cachet* confine him in a secret dungeon "at the king's pleasure."

Another active cause of discontent was the stupid and oppressive legislation which fettered the expanding trade and industry of the age. Interior customs lines restricted the normal flow of commodities, feudal overlords still levied toll on certain goods passing through their dominions, and town wardens stopped merchandise at the gate for an entrance fee. In industry progress was checked by the obstructive and antiquated guilds, which guarded their monopolies jealously. Artisans were forbidden to change from, one trade to another, and better and speedier methods of manufacture were frequently outlawed because of ancient ordinances which had outlived whatever usefulness they once possessed.

Had the government of Louis XV pursued an energetic and successful policy abroad, Frenchmen might have overlooked their domestic ills. But in the wars of the eighteenth century, France was singularly unfortunate; by 1763 the country had lost all but a remnant of its colonial empire, and amassed a heavy debt. Frenchmen knew that their country was one of the most populous, fertile, and wealthy in Europe, yet every year they saw the national indebtedness increase, until bankers hesitated to lend money to the state even at twenty per cent interest. One grave fault of the fiscal system was the custom known as "farming out the taxes." A group of wealthy men would advance a sum of money to the king in exchange for his permission to reimburse them by collecting the taxes due. As they collected more than they turned in, this practice of discounting the revenue meant that it was carried to the king as it were in a leaking bucket. A second grave fault was the absence of a budget. The monarch treated the national revenues as a private credit account, and could squander upon his mistresses and his amusements the resources which should have been devoted to urgent national needs (Ibid.).

Eminent *Philosophes* or Philosophers

Francois Marie Arouet, better known as Voltaire (1694-1778), the most famous of the *philosophes,* made Europe a court which rang with his appeals. He was the self-appointed champion of all victims of bigotry and injustice. Against the theologians in particular, he delighted to turn the flood of his mockery. He believed that religion had originated long before priests, but it had been exploited ever since "the first knave met the first fool." Insistently he raised the battle cry, *Ecrasez l'infame!* (Destroy the infamous thing!), for to him intolerance symbolized all that was stupid, irrational, and degrading in the old regime. He pointed out that a "natural religion" was one that would "enjoin us" to serve our neighbours through love of God," but we had been led by intolerance and bigotry into the monstrous error of "persecuting and butchering them to His greater glory" (quoted in Ferguson 1958: 591).

Baron de Montesquieu (1689-1755) writings had considerable influence. Although he had been trained to the practice of the law, he chose to study the origin and nature of government. His greatest work, *L'Esprit des Lois* (The Spirit of the Laws) was published in 1748. Like most political theorists of the eighteenth century he observed that much existing legislation was unwise and irrational because it did not rest on a natural and logical foundation. He argued, "Laws, in the broadest sense, are indispensable relationships implicit in the nature of things." He believed that political liberty could best be preserved if the executive, legislative, and judicial branches of a government were separated and kept in equilibrium. This doctrine of "the separation of powers" did not originate with Montesquieu, but he gave it a new definition and a new emphasis (Ibid.: 591).

Denis Diderot (1713-1784), who edited an *Encyclopedia, or Methodical Dictionary of the Sciences, Arts and Trades* to which almost all the *philosophes* contributed. While avoiding controversial subjects as far as possible, the encyclopedists wrote to convince the thoughtful reader that science and the growth of a tolerant spirit had contributed more to the happiness of mankind than the tenets of a thousand warring religious faiths. This famous encyclopaedia proved an arsenal of arguments for the rationalist cause and was completed in 1765 in spite of repeated efforts by the clergy and the censors to suppress it.

Marquis Beccaria (1738-1794), an Italian *philosophe,* in his *An Essay on Crimes and Punishments* (1764) wrote against the inequality of the laws, and the immunities enjoyed by the privileged orders. He denounced the use of torture and the infliction of cruel and outmoded punishments. He was against the spectacle of criminal going to execution which he considered as a constant reminder of the barbarous codes in force. He even ventured to urge the abolition of the death penalty, arguing that "crimes are more effectively prevented by the *certainty* than the *severity* of the punishment."

Francois Quesnay (1694-1774), court physician to Louis XV, became the leader of a group of thinkers known as the *physiocrats.* They believed all governments should conform to "the natural order of things." They regarded most legislation as a curse rather than a benefit insisting that trade, for instance, developed most vigorously when least interfered with, since artificial regulations constricted it. Hence, their slogan was "to govern better, govern less." The mercantilist theory that a state grew wealthy by accumulating gold they declared unsound; the wealth of a society was the *produit net*, the surplus of agricultural, mineral, and other natural products accruing from the labour of its citizens. Agriculture they considered the most vital interest of a nation and they believed it important to improve the lot of the French peasantry because "poor peasants make a poor kingdom." There must be a *natural* order of society, the principles of which had been lost or ignored, and it was the business of the legislators to regenerate society by discovering and applying these natural principles. Once enunciated, the new precepts would be accepted by all right-thinking people. Some of these natural and axiomatic laws the *philosophes* believed they had already discovered, but they lacked the authority to put them into force. They sought, therefore, to persuade the princes of Europe to employ their despotic authority to inaugurate reforms and remould society to a fairer pattern.

Reforms under Enlightened Despots

In 1768 Diderot declared enthusiastically, "There is no prince in Europe who is not also a philosopher" (quoted in Ferguson 1958:593). And many of the princes did attempt to reform the socio-economic conditions. They read the criticisms of the *philosophes*, discussed reform programmes with their advisers, and dreamed of using their royal power to carry through "a revolution from above." Their *aims* were often admirable; they wanted to introduce greater order and clarity in government and jurisprudence, to make their countries stronger and more prosperous, their subjects happier, and themselves more popular. The *philosophes* encouraged and flattered these reforming monarchs, assuring them that "a philosopher on a throne" was the noblest type of ruler. A philosopher-prince, they insisted, if he were wise and firm, could influence an entire society by the example and his edicts, and infuse all the branches of his government with his own spirit – the spirit of wisdom, power, and benevolence. Thus, monarchy was given a last chance to justify itself as "enlightened despotism." The European rulers of the later eighteenth century were for the most part earnest and well-meaning princes. In recognition of their high sense of responsibility, and their sincere desire to improve the lot of their subjects, they have been styled the "enlightened despots" and the middle and later years of the eighteenth century constitute "the monarchs' age of repentance." These princes strove to undo in one century the mistakes their ancestors had committed in five. Had they succeeded, benevolent despotism might still be accepted as the ideal form of government in Europe, but their intelligence was not equal to their intentions, and several of them, in their attempts to improve matters, ended by making them worse.

The most sincere and least successful of benevolent princes was the Emperor Joseph II of Austria (1780-90). "Joseph always wishes to take the second step before he has taken the first," was the shrewd judgment of Frederick the Great. In Spain the conscientious Charles III (1759-88) curbed the power of the Inquisition and expelled the Jesuits from the kingdom (1767). In Portugal under Pombal, minister of Joseph I (1750-77) secured the expulsion of the Jesuits from Portugal in 1759, and the Society of Jesus, which had become unpopular, was suppressed by a papal decree in 1773. In Sweden, Gustavus III (1771-92), the versatile monarch possessed a magnetic personality and laboured with zest to reform the finances, improve agriculture, promote education and religious tolerance, and ameliorate the harshness of the laws. Unfortunately, he excited the opposition of various privileged groups, and in 1792 he was assassinated by some discontented nobles. In Denmark-Norway, Count Struensee, able minister of the king, Christian VII, likewise paid with his life for his presumptuous attempts to play the enlightened despot. As the power behind the throne from 1771 to 1772, Struensee reorganized the administration and attacked everything that was corrupt in the state of Denmark, until his enemies combined to impeach him and send him to the block. But the memory of his reforms survived him, for legitimate ideals and aspirations are more difficult to silence than their mortal advocates.

In France, the accession of Louis XVI in 1774 brought a promise of better days, for one of his first acts was to appoint the wise and courageous Turgot, controller general of the finances. Turgot was a friend of the *philosophes* and favoured many of the reforms which they had proposed. "Give me five years of despotism," he proposed, "and France shall be free." The danger of insolvency he met with the bold policy: "No bankruptcy, no increase in taxation, no loans." Only a rigid curtailment of expenditures could make the plan a success, yet, when Turgot attempted to introduce economies in order to balance the budget, he created a host of enemies from the extravagant young queen, Marie Antoinette, to the holder of the smallest sinecure. Had Louis XVI supported him firmly, he might have fought his way through, but in 1776 his enemies won the king over and Turgot was dismissed after twenty months in office. His final prophetic plea was, "Do not forget, sire, that it was weakness which brought the head of Charles I to the block" (quoted in Ferguson 1958: 595). But Louis was too confused and too irresolute to profit by sage advice. Turgot's fall sealed the fate of the French monarchy, for under his successors in office the old expedients were revived, new loans were floated, expenditures increased, and the ship of state drifted steadily toward the rocks of revolution. When intelligent Frenchmen saw the king and his ministers delay so long in carrying through the needed reforms, they began to ask themselves whether there was not some other authority in the state to which they might appeal. They knew that in the previous century the English people had grown impatient with their monarchy, had sent

Charles I to execution, and later had driven James II from his throne and kingdom. These acts had shocked Europe in an age when almost everyone accepted the principle of the divine right of kings, and the English revolutionists had endeavoured to justify their unconventional procedure. In 1789, in France, the leaders of the middle class prepared to sweep away the old regime with its inequalities and abuses, but they ended by sweeping away the French monarchy also, and plunged their newly proclaimed republic into a war with the rest of Europe.

Views of John Locke (1632-1704) and Jean Jacques Rousseau (1712-1778)

John Locke did not originate the idea of the sovereignty of the people, but he was one of the first writers to present it clearly and make it popular. Any people desiring to throw off allegiance to an unpopular monarch could now find an argument to justify the act. He argued very reasonably that governments were instituted by the people to protect their lives and property; that when a government failed to fulfil these functions, or a king abused his power, the sovereign people had the right to change their government for a better one. This was what the English had done in 1688-89 when they expelled the absolutist James II and invited William and Mary to rule in his place as constitutional monarchs. They found comfort in Locke's doctrine, which assured them that, far from being rebels, they had in fact acted as honest and courageous citizens defending their natural rights. In the American War of Independence, the "patriots" invoked Locke's philosophy to prove that the tyranny of George III had absolved the colonists from their allegiance to the English king, and that they were asserting no more than their "natural rights" in setting up an independent government. The idea that the people were not created to obey the king, but that kings were merely executive magistrates responsible to the sovereign people, was indeed a revolutionary concept.

In France, where it was to precipitate the greatest revolution of all, the new philosophy found an eloquent advocate in one of the most moving and passionate spirits of the century, Jean Jacques Rousseau (1712-78). He first achieved fame as a writer in Paris when he composed a prize essay in 1749. He followed this with several works wherein he attacked the evils of society and government, not coldly and rationally as more philosophical critics had done, but with a fresh and emotional style that charmed his readers. In *The Social Contract* (1762) he formulated his philosophy of government, and pictured the state as a corporate body of citizens who subordinate their individual aims to the "general will." The sovereign power resides in the citizens, but it is indivisible, and the government derives its authority from the consent of the governed. This was a radical doctrine to preach in a country where the king supposedly ruled by divine right. How radical it was, he made clear by his further statement that "the depositaries of the executive power are not the people's masters but its officers ... it can set them up or pull them down when it likes." And the seeds of revolution were inherent in Rousseau's pronouncement that "Man is born free; and everywhere he is in chains."

How deeply Rousseau's political ideas influenced French opinion before 1789 is a matter of dispute. Earlier, he was regarded as "the author who above all others, inspired the French Revolution," but more recent studies suggest that *The Social Contract* was not widely read in France until after the Revolution began. There can be no doubt, however, that the attitude of the French people toward their government became increasingly critical in the later eighteenth century. Whether they drew arguments from Rousseau, from the writings of the *philosophes*, or from general discussions does not greatly matter. The important point is that by 1789 there was a widespread conviction that reforms were urgently needed. The critics of the old regime had set ideas circulating through men's minds, ideas that, like a subtle acid, dissolved the presuppositions upon which the old regime rested. So deep was the general dissatisfaction, so widespread the desire for reform, that one eminent historian has ventured to declare: "The Revolution was accomplished in men's minds before they made it the work of their hands" (Ibid.: 597).

Case of the American Revolution (1776)

The news from American that the people of the Thirteen Colonies had thrown off the rule of a king and set up a republic provided a further incentive to the French to undertake radical reforms. For as De Tocqueville later observed, "The Americans appeared to carry out what our own writers had prefigured. They gave the substance of reality to our dreams" (quoted in Ferguson 1958: 597). Therefore, it will be appropriate to analyze to what extent the leaders who drafted a constitution and organized a government for the United States of America were influenced by the ideas that were circulating in Europe at the time.

To achieve unity amid diversity, organize a representative government, reconcile liberty with authority, regulate taxation, commerce, and currency, govern the western lands, and maintain forces adequate for defence – all these problems confronted the leaders of the United States of America after peace was signed in 1783. While fighting for independence all thirteen states had formed an alliance under Articles of Confederation which were too loose, too imprecise, to implement a genuine national government with power to levy taxes, enforce the laws, and regulate commerce. In 1787, therefore, a convention of delegates from the several states met in Philadelphia and drew up a constitution which it was hoped would prove "adequate to the exigencies of the Union." The constitution thus devised was ratified in 1788 and George Washington took office as first President of the United States in 1789.

The framers of the Constitution may not have been the "assemblage of demigods" that Jefferson termed them, but they were exceptionally gifted and farseeing statesmen and they proved it by the solutions they found for three major problems. Firstly, by adopting the principle of federalism they left each component state a large measure of independence but reserved for a national government the powers essential to it – the authority to levy taxes, regulate trade, control western lands and adjust disputes between the states and the citizens of different states. Secondly, by declaring that "this Constitution, and the laws of the United States which shall be made in pursuance there of" were "the Supreme Law of the Land," the framers made it enforceable on all citizens. Thirdly, by providing for a "separation of powers" they made it possible for the executive, legislative, and judicial branches of the Federal Government to evolve with a relative independence that prevented any one of them from attaining a preponderant influence. The elaborate "checks and balances" established by the Constitution, though cumbrous, were designed to safeguard the rights and liberties of the people and to protect them against abuse of power by those whom they placed in office. As a further safeguard, ten amendments were added to the original

Constitution to stipulate still more explicitly the rights of individual citizens and of the component states. This "Bill of rights" came into effect in 1791.

Critics of the old regime in Europe noted that the Americans had borrowed and applied many of the principles advocated by the *philosophes*. In some instances, indeed, they had adopted solutions more venturesome and radical than most Europeans were yet ready to accept. Nevertheless the ideals set forth in the American Declaration of Independence, the Federal Constitution, and the Bill of Rights encouraged European reformers. For the Americans dared to affirm that all men are created equal, that they have an unalienable right to life, liberty, and the pursuit of happiness, that governments are instituted to assure these rights and derive their just powers from the consent of the governed. When the Americans embodied these ideals in a written constitution, and assigned the executive, legislative, and judicial functions of their federal government to three separate departments it seemed clear that they had profited by studying the writings of Locke and Montesquieu. When they abolished cruel and unusual punishments and framed a judicial code to promote equal justice under law, it likewise seemed that they had heeded the protests levelled by Beccaria, Voltaire, and others against cruel and unjust laws. When they separated church and state, they made it clear that they favoured freedom of religious worship.

SCIENCE AND SOCIETY IN THE TWENTIETH CENTURY

Since 1871 the rapid industrial development was stimulated by new and revolutionary advances in science and technology. As a result, industry superseded agriculture as the main source of livelihood for a majority of the people in the industrialized states. But this extension of the factory system deepened the conflict between the owners of the machines and the workers, while the steady accumulation of capital and the need for raw materials drove the powers to exploit so-called backward countries and expand their colonial empires. As a consequence the period from 1871 to 1914 witnessed social conflicts and the rise of socialist parties within the industrialized states, and keener commercial and colonial competitions among European powers. This phase is, thus, characterized as an age of new industrialism and imperialism.

In these years also, two new world powers were emerging outside the European political sphere. The United States, whose civilization had been European, or Western, since its inception was rapidly becoming one of the leading industrial states. Japan, grafting Western ways onto its ancient Oriental culture, was transforming itself into a modern state with incredible speed and was bidding for the dominant role in Asian affairs. Meanwhile, Asians were growing increasingly resentful of European imperialism. But up to 1914 these forces were still peripheral, and the key to Europe's immediate future remained in Europe's own hands. As the tension increased among the European powers, they were driven into two competing systems of alliances, while the people suffered the burden of ever increasing armaments. A succession of diplomatic crises culminated, in 1914, in the outbreak of a tragic and destructive war.

The March of Science

The chief factor underlying the dynamic changes has been the progress of science and industry. Earlier chapters described the beginnings of the modern science in the sixteenth and seventeenth centuries, the advances in mathematical method, and the brilliant discoveries in astronomy, physics, and other fields of investigation. The scientists of the eighteenth century extended and systematized this new knowledge with such success that they made their period an age of reason and a scientific renaissance. But not until the nineteenth century did the fruits of their researches really make themselves felt in the life of the common man (Ibid.: 739).

The introduction of the steamship and the railway a century ago shrank this planet so surprisingly that distant continents became more accessible than neighbouring states had been a few decades earlier. As a result, Europe was able to lay the world under contribution, drawing the products of every clime and every continent to her ports. The Atlantic Cable reaches Newfoundland in 1866. The newspaper folded beside his plate likewise bears witness to a revolution in communication. From every part of the world the events of the previous twenty-four hours have been leaned for his entertainment and information. In 1892, Alexander Graham Bell made the first telephone call between New York and Chicago. The more recent devices of wireless telegraphy, radio, and television are already accepted as commonplaces by people whose tastes are jaded with so many scientific wonders. The production of iron, an essential commodity of the machine age, increased a hundred-fold in the nineteenth century, and the output of coal kept pace with it. New inventions, such as the internal combustion engine, created new demands, and the world production of petroleum after 1900 leaped ahead one thousand per cent in thirty years. To satisfy the insatiable demands of expanding industries men learned to tap pools of oil miles below the earth's crust, to draw nitrogen from the atmosphere, and to extract bromine from the sea. Power for their engines was obtained by a reckless consumption of coal, oil, or gas, or by harnessing the tireless waterfalls.

Nor did science lag in finding new ways to augment the food supply for the hungry millions. By the use of fertilizers, by experimenting with new and more nutritious types of grains and fruits, by the invention of agricultural machinery, power-driven ploughs, tractors, and threshing machines, the world's food supply has been rapidly increased. By means of refrigerator cars and steamers millions of tons of fruit or meat can now be shipped from continent to continent, or, sealed in sterilized cans, may be preserved for years until need. The dread spectre of famine which had lurked on the edge of every human community since the beginning of history seemed about to withdraw as the twentieth century opened. Man had abundance in his grasp, though he had not learned to use it wisely or to conserve its sources.

This increase in material wealth has made the world a vastly more luxurious and amusing place for many people. Today the citizen of modest circumstances can afford luxuries which a Roman noble could not obtain with a thousand slaves. The electric light, telephone, and radio, the steamship, train and automobile are at the disposal of millions. "The Ceasars carried no timepiece as accurate as a five-dollar watch, nor could their banquet table provide the variety of flavours obtainable at a modern soda fountain. Silk, once the apparel of princes, has become a household article, and materials unknown or unprocurable to the ancients, such as rustless steel, aluminium, rubber and a hundred synthetic products, are cheaply available to all" (Ibid.: 740-42).

The New Environment: The Civilization of City Dwellers

The acceleration of the forces shaping modern life – the flood of inventions and the multi-fold discoveries – grew so rapid that it really constituted a second industrial revolution or what might better, perhaps, be termed a Technological Revolution (Ibid.: 746). Successive innovations, such as the automobile, the motion picture, the airplane, and the radio led to the establishment of new industries almost overnight. They required hundreds of thousands of workers and were centred often in mushroom cities created to house their plants and their employees. The new methods of quantity production necessitated the coordination of all the processes of an industry, and of associated trades, so that the garment makers tended to congregate in one locality, the makers of automobile parts in another. Since machines required power to run them and raw materials to feed them, it was most profitable to establish factories where these essentials were easily available. Thus, in selecting the site of operations the machine was the master, and the workmen who had to tend it were condemned to live nearby. Too often this meant that thousands of mill hands had to pass their lives under the smoke-laden sky of a factory town, where the grass withered from the fumes of the blast furnaces and the streams were polluted with the wastage of tanks and vats. The migration of the population toward the new industrial centres, a shift already observable in England at the close of the eighteenth century, continued at an increasing rate throughout the nineteenth in all the leading European countries.

The result was the growth of cities at the expense of the country districts. The most notable feature about the population in the modern industrial state is the fact that it is predominantly an urban population. Until a century ago, and even later, the people of the British Isles, France, or Germany lived chiefly on the land, supporting them by some form of agricultural labour. England was the first state to discover, about 1850, that the town dwellers had grown to outnumber the country folk. In France and Germany the same phenomenon was observed, induced by the same causes.

It follows that the proper regulation and development of those cities in which so large a part of the people live must be of pressing concern to modern governments. Cities are vast agglomerations of unique and artificial growth. To police them, to safeguard their thousands or millions of inhabitants, to direct their traffic and dispose of their refuse, employs an army of public servants. Many modern cities have grown up so hurriedly and haphazardly that vast sums must later be expended to provide an adequate water supply, to create port and railway facilities, playgrounds, parks, and traffic speedways. A little foresight and foreknowledge might have solved many problems in advance, but the rapid changes of the machine era took governments by surprise and found even the experts largely unprepared.

Thus, the advancement in communication, the revival of commerce, and the growth of the towns raised a new class to prominence, the class of manufacturers, bankers, and traders. The wealth of these men was not in land, but in the commodities they sold, in bills of exchange, and in money. Though scorned at first by the feudal, landowning nobles, the merchant class gained steadily in power and wealth and influence. In time this emerging middle class became strong enough to challenge the privileged position of the feudal aristocracy, and in the end they succeeded, with the aid of the seventeenth-century revolutions in England and the great revolution in France, in dominating state policies. By 1832, the bourgeoisie, the class composed of manufacturers, merchants, traders, bankers, professional men, and shopkeepers, had secured control of the government in France and Great Britain.

After the middle of the nineteenth century, the deepening antagonism between the capitalist employers and the workingmen acquired new significance through the writings of Karl Marx. Born in Trier, Germany, Marx enjoyed an excellent education, but his political activities got him into trouble in his homeland and also in France. He took an active part in the revolution of 1848 in Germany, after which he settled in London in order to devote himself to study and to the development of those theories which have earned him the title "the father of modern socialism." He formulated a new philosophy of history, based upon his conclusion that the factor which is common to society in every age is the exploitation of one class by another. In modern society, he found this "class struggle" exemplified in the contest between capital and labour, the capitalists being the "expropriators" and the workingmen the "expropriated," and he prophesied that the struggle would gradually split society into two hostile camps with no middle ground between. For him, the progress of the Industrial Revolution seemed destined to multiply the profits of the machine-owners while the proletarians grew more numerous and more conscious of their violated rights. In the end, he prophesied, the proletariat would take over the machinery of production to run it for the benefit of all, and the "expropriators" would be expropriated.

In 1864, socialists from various countries attempted to organize an international movement for which Marx prepared a constitution. Weakened by the desertion of the moderates and the expulsion of the anarchists, this First International foundered in 1874, but a Second International was formed in 1889. Meanwhile, socialist groups in the leading European countries entered the political arena and socialist voters polled an increasing number of ballots. By 1914, the Socialist parties in France and Germany had each over a hundred deputies in parliament, while in the British House of Commons the Labour Party held forty seats. Thus, the spread of democracy in the period 1870-1914 and the extension of the suffrage to all classes naturally favoured the expansion of the socialist parties. Their leaders hoped a time would soon come when the workers, as the most numerous class in each state, would control the parliaments through the deputies whom they elected, for when they secured this control they could transform the capitalist system by legislative decrees. All moderate-minded men hoped that the ends of social justice might be realized by constitutional means and the problems growing out of the class struggle would find an *evolutionary* rather than a *revolutionary* solution. The parliaments of the nineteenth century had generally avoided these problems, and, true to the bourgeois doctrine of *laissez faire*, or "let alone," they had left the workers to the mercy of their employers. But there seemed good reason to hope after 1900 that the parliaments of the twentieth century would abandon this evasive course and grapple honestly with the task of reconciling the demands of capital and labour. Unhappily, this hope was to be jeopardized by the outbreak of two world wars and a succession of later small wars and disturbances which threatened democratic governments everywhere.

Like the "class struggle," the world wars were very largely a product of the new forces which science and industry had let loose in society. The economic rivalries of imperialistic powers which helped to provoke war, the machine guns, submarine boats, and poison gas which multiplied its horrors, and the aircraft which dropped bombs on vulnerable cities were no less the products of the new world science and industry provided than the cheap food, the rapid transportation, and the protection against plagues. The Industrial Revolution not only helped to intensify the class struggle within the modern states; it also helped to intensify the jealousies existing among the modern states (Ibid.: 747-49).

The great power competition amongst the industrialized State and the new imperialism led to the Second World War. Subsequently, the stream of history underwent another of those almost indefinable changes that signal the end of one era and the beginning of another. This change had of course been a long time in the making. The scientific and intellectual character of our time as well as its technical achievements was a growth deep rooted in the whole course of Western civilization, but it has taken on a new quality with the dawn of the nuclear age, as man faces up to the fateful task of seeing to it that his destructive powers do not overbalance his constructive genius, that his control over natural forces does not outrun his control of himself.

Politically, the years after 1939 witnessed the emergence of a new global balance of power. The Second World War further weakened European influence in world affairs and left the United States and Soviet Russia the leaders of two great opposing social and political systems. The defeat of Japan and Germany had created vacuums into which Communist influence penetrated, and although the United Nations organization offered a new means and hope of international cooperation, the polarization of world tensions between the communist and the capitalist nations threatened to limit its usefulness. To offset the military and ideological threat of the Communist bloc, therefore, the United States abandoned its policy of avoiding foreign entanglements and took the lead in forming a North Atlantic Treaty Organization which strengthened the western European states by assuring them American arms and aid if they were attacked; and though eastern and middle Europe had been absorbed into the Soviet orbit by the end war, the tide of Communist expansion toward the west was stemmed. But in Asia, communism advanced more relentlessly, in a pragmatic alliance with the aspirations of the Asian peoples toward national self-determination.

SCIENCE, MODERNITY AND SOCIAL RESEARCH

Tremendous accumulations of factual knowledge in every branch of inquiry have opened new doors to the speculative intellect, and new hypotheses and theories have given rise in turn to further investigation and experiment. As knowledge has grown, new branches of exiting sciences have come into being. Thus what once was "just chemistry" is now physical chemistry, organic chemistry, bio-chemistry, and so on. Besides "plain physics" there are geophysics, astrophysics, and nuclear physics. Knowledge, once looked upon as a single stream, was divided in the seventeenth century because no one man could any longer compass it all. The division has continued; yet in another sense the branches of the stream have merged again, not because it is easier to grasp all knowledge, but because it has been found that the branches flow together once more. A biologist, for instance cannot study metabolism, digestion, or cell structure, without knowing a good deal of chemistry; a chemist cannot deal with the forces in the nucleus of the atom without working also in physics.

But the domain of science has grown beyond the study of the world of nature. The key methods of the natural sciences – experiment, the gathering and analysis of data, and the formulation and testing of hypotheses – have also been applied to whole areas of once non-scientific study; to the mind (psychology and psychiatry); the structure of society (sociology and anthropology); the economic system; and even such rather remote areas as the nature of language, the canon of books in the Bible, and the principles of literary criticism. Indeed, so potent today is the name of science that faith in its methods and findings sometimes approaches the unscientific, in a tendency to deny that there are areas of investigation in which scientific methods may not be the only applicable ones

This wave of scientific interest came about from a variety of causes, some of which, as we have seen, arose as early as the seventeenth century with the work of Francis Bacon, who first enunciated the experimental method, Robert Boyle, the father of modern chemistry, Sir Isaac Newton, the founder of modern physics, and the members of the Royal Society who after 1660 poled their knowledge and experiments to derive the greatest benefit for the confraternity from the work of each. In the three centuries from Bacon to 1900, it had been amply proved that scientific investigation uncovers hitherto unknown facts and leads to verifiable results. Then two things happened in the later nineteenth century which gave the scientific method greater impetus than it had ever received before. One of these was philosophical; the propounding of Darwin's theory of evolution. The other was practical: the pressure of an expanding industrial economy for improvements in technology. It would be easy to speculate that the first of these developments affected pure science and the second applied science. But it is hardly realistic to separate pure from applied science, for each stimulates the other and depends heavily upon the other. Both depend on outside factors such as economic or humanitarian need, money, time, equipment for research, and the great imponderable – talent. Yet it cannot be denied that the later nineteenth and early twentieth century gave rise to a number of ideas, theories, and discoveries in pure science that have been since not only worked out in greater detail, but often also applied to practical end (Ibid.: 920-21).

Through all this ferment of thought and discovery there has been constant stimulus and interplay between science and technology, often increased by economic pressure from industry and finance. As early as 1856, growing railroads needed better steel, and the Bessemer process provided it. Increasing trade, growing populations, and the rising tempo of life put hard pressure on communications, and inventors responded with the telegraph, the Atlantic cable, the telephone and radio by the end of nineteenth century. Illumination, once only by candle or oil, then briefly by gas, had Edison's incandescent bulb by 1879; and with the tremendous demand for electric power which it created, came the need for better generating plants, dynamos, transformers, and power lines. Electric energy, generated by steam or water power, sped over high-tension wires to illuminate cities and farms, operate factories and railroads, and run an ever-increasing number of mechanical devices. Another source of power, the internal combustion engine, was invented at the close of the nineteenth century. It made the automobile possible, thus giving rise to the gigantic automotive industry and revolutionizing transportation; it sped the mechanization of agriculture and brought more acres under cultivation through the use of power-driven farm equipment; and because it could deliver more power to its weight than the steam engine, it finally enabled man to conquer the air. A scant, half-century after Orville and Wilbur Wright achieved the first successful powered flights at Kitty Hawk, North Carolina, in 1903, regularly scheduled air flights were spanning the continents and the oceans of the earth.

This relatively simple view of the atom has since been greatly refined, but even in its early form it pointed to a revolutionary new concept of the nature of matter and energy. In the older physics, matter was conceived to be one thing and energy another, and as we have seen, matter was believed to be indestructible, though it could be changed in form, with each body in the universe attracting every other by a force which depended on their size and distance from each other. But in 1905, partly as the result of the growing knowledge of radioactivity and atomic structure, Albert Einstein (1879-1955) proposed in his famous formula, $E=mc^2$, the theory that matter and energy are simply different manifestations of the same thing: that *matter is energy*. It had been noted that radium, as it disintegrates, gives forth very large amounts of energy. According to Einstein's formula the destruction of a single gram of matter (it takes nearly 350 grams to make an ounce) would yield as much energy as the burning of 23,000 tons of coal.

Only forty years after Einstein announced his mass-energy formula, it found its most striking application. In 1945 the world was stunned by the explosion of the first atomic bombs, releasing tremendous forces by the transformation of matter into energy. It was also the troubled dawn of a new era in history, the age of atomic or nuclear energy. The new sources of power thus made available had great potentialities for peaceful enterprise, but their wartime possibilities were so tremendous that they set off a new kind of armaments race which in the years since has helped to divide the world into hostile camps. In some ways the conquest of the atom seemed a curse and not a blessing. To thoughtful people in many lands, it looked as if man had learned to control physical nature before he had mastered himself.

After the concept of biological evolution placed man himself within the compass of the sciences, it was natural that he should turn to the scientific method, which had served him so well in the physical world, to attempt a better understanding and control of his relations with his fellows and with his environment. By the twentieth century, science and technology were moving ahead so rapidly that in addition to such inherited social problems as urban housing, industrial working conditions, unemployment, and the distribution of wealth, mankind now faced the immense and ever present task of adjusting to a constantly changing environment. New inventions like television, new concepts of the relation between space and time as practically dramatized in air travel, new folkways like those opened up by the automobile, and new conditions of existence itself, like nuclear fission and the hydrogen bomb, had to be assimilated almost overnight. And the perplexities of environmental adjustment were further multiplied by the fact that not all groups and societies in the modern world had reached the same stage of material development.

To these problems of betterment and adjustment the new "social sciences" offered a promising approach. They provided a systematic means of dealing with the mass of data and the bewildering variety of phenomena of a society whose processes had been rendered complex by modern technology and whose interrelationships had been multiplied by modern means of communication. Economics, raised from the field of speculation to that of science by the systematic accumulation of data and the testing of hypotheses, tackled such problems as the distribution of economic goods, they "boom and bust" cycles of economic activity, and the conflict of national economic interests. Anthropology, by the concrete and critical observation of primitive cultures, brought new insights to bear on the forces at work in civilized society. Sociology (the term was originated by Auguste Comte in 1838), the most comprehensive of all the social sciences, sought to provide man with a scientific means of stabilizing the dynamic world he inhabited and of achieving some measure of responsible social control over it.

The most formidable adjustment that science and technology demanded of western society was the transition from a rural agrarian to an urban-industrial environment. Twentieth-century man, at least in the technically more advanced segments of society, tended to live and work in cities, where were clustered the factories and office buildings of an industrial society. Similarly, man's relation to his community underwent a change as the nerve-centre of his life moved from the ploughed field to the assembly line. City-dweller or suburbanite, he stood in a less intimate, less urgent and individual relation to the place where he worked and lived than did the townsman or countryman of an earlier day. Again, the standardization and mechanization of many tasks in a mass-production economy deprived the worker of the pride in creative accomplishment that the husbandman or artisan once experienced. A loss of identity, a rootlessness and restlessness, a sense of insecurity, afflicted urban man and created that twentieth-century phenomenon, the "lonely crowd" – the masses of people who lived without significance of fulfilment in a world from which they felt alienated. Their lives had become longer, safer, healthier, and in many material respects richer than those of their forefathers; but all were haunted by vague fears of man-made forces beyond their individual control, of unemployment or of nuclear destruction. Science and technology, which have given modern man so much, have not always offered adequate substitutes for what they have taken away (Ibid.: 927-28).

It would not be wrong to say that the social research emerged out of the epistemological optimism put forward by the Enlightenment philosophers. Since inception, it was guided by these two philosophic foundations: objective and universal science, and progressive and historically inevitable modernity. For a scientific study of society it differentiated itself from religion, metaphysics and commonsense in its quest for an objective, value neutral and empirical science. Also, it evolved itself, from time to time, in order to make sense of the new age. As evident, the leading social researchers of the late nineteenth and early twentieth century, from Auguste Comte to Karl Marx, were the children of modernity. In their own specific ways, they celebrated the new age and wrote substantially about it. They were great scholars, and immensely sensitive. They could see the pathologies of modernity. For example, Durkheim was concerned about anomies: the growing normlessness in modern societies. Marx was a great humanist who critiqued the fragmented character of capitalism, and its alienation. Max Weber spoke of the pathos of disenchantment inherent in the modern age. But, even when they saw problems with modernity, they did not want to regress to a non-modern age. Instead, they retained their faith in the foundations of modernity and science, and sought to accomplish the agenda of modernity by making it more humane and egalitarian.

Science with its central principles of objectivity, universalization and causal explanation did have a tremendous impact on the formation of modern social science and its methodology. However, there was not absolute agreement on the "unity of method." True, positivism, a dominant mode of sociological enquiry in the nineteenth and early twentieth century, did not see much qualitative difference in the study of nature and socio-cultural domain. But then, there were many who differed, and pleaded for a separate mode of enquiry in social and cultural sciences. Its roots could be seen in Immanuel Kant (1724-1804) who postulated two distinct principles, firstly, the physical component being enslaved by the senses, and secondly, the moral component that strives for truth, justice and beauty. No wonder, one aspect of the Enlightenment social theory that spoke of human beings' conditioning gave birth to material and structural analysis, and the other mode of enquiry that spoke of human beings' freedom gave importance to voluntarism, human agency, creativity and reflexivity.

There are social scientists who would argue that unlike an object in the physico-chemical or biological world, the human being is a creative and reflexive creature, and human society is, therefore, a domain of meanings, not just an "external thing" constraining us. In other words, human society, it is argued, has to be seen as a product of creative accomplishment on the part of the social actors. The task of social research is to understand and interpret these meanings. Max Weber emerged out of this philosophic tradition. For Weber (1949), social research is an interpretative study of the subjective meaning complex of social actions. He regarded it as *verstehen*, a method of understanding the conscious and subjective meanings social actors attach to the world. It was in this sense that Weber saw beyond mere economism, and interpreted early capitalism as a domain of meanings that the proponents of Protestantism or Calvinism attached to the world. Well, Weber did speak of the human agency. But this does not mean that his sociology was "subjective" in nature. Instead, he sought to unite the interpretative study of subjective meanings with an objective causal analysis. He was not against the basic tenets of science: objectivity, value neutrality and causal explanation. What he was objecting to was the positivist urge to equate society with nature, and undermine the domain of meanings. He was therefore talking about 'ideal types' which were more like models rather than exact scientific laws.

In the twentieth and early twenty first century the tradition of interpretative social research was further developed through phenomenological and ethno-methodological traditions. The central thrust of these traditions is that the world is largely a world experienced by human beings and the task of social researchers is to describe, understand and make sense of this world: how people themselves define and construct it. Alfred Schutz (1899-1959), a major proponent of the phenomenological tradition, spoke of the inter-subjective world in which people interact, communicate and understand one another through the process of typification, that is to say, a process that enables people to fix and define one another and have a shared role-expectation. It is through this process of typification that a meaningful and stable social order is possible. For Schutz (1972) the everyday world in which people interact is the paramount reality. It is taken for granted. And that makes society possible. But then, there are other realms, like the realm of dreams, or the realm of scientific theorizing, in which people experience the world. All these finite provinces of meaning have their own notions of time and space, and shifts from one realm to the other involve 'shock'. But then, for Schutz, the paramount reality is most important, and all of us have to come back to it and experience the world as direct and real actors. Social research, for Schutz, must describe and understand how people experience the world. This means that social research must take people's descriptions and definitions seriously. Likewise, Harold Garfinkel (1967) spoke of ethno-methodology, or 'people's methodology'. The task is to describe how people themselves define their world, not to explain it in terms of some context-free, abstract, universal generalization. In other words, social research has witnessed a shift from abstract explanation to meaningful understanding, from universality to specificity, from theory to description, from structural causes to people's lived experiences.

The two traditions of social research, positivist and interpretative, have a point of convergence, because both these traditions emerged out of the Enlightenment modernity. In the positivist tradition, we could see the Enlightenment affirmation of the legitimacy of scientific explanation. And in the interpretative tradition we could find the affirmation of the Enlightenment optimism centred on human beings' agency and their ability to create their own world. But then, as we have discussed, these very foundations are in a crisis, since all these modern principles, scientific objectivity, historical progress, coherent and rational self, and the agency and freedom of the actor, are doubted, particularly with the advent of post modernity. And it has caused a severe philosophic crisis, and social science research has to cope with it. For post modernists, there is no foundational truth that can prove to be objective, there is no universal and totalizing theory that can overcome local contexts and heterogeneity, and there is no "superior" method like science or positivism. Post modernity asserts that there is no universal truth, there is no culture that can claim itself to be superior to others, and the world is a site of differences. In other words, for postmodernists, there is no grand truth on science, progress and modernity. Instead, there are multiple voices, and the very notion of a rational and coherent subject is questioned.

However, there are many reasons for the disillusionment with the project of modernity. The experience of war, violence and totalitarianism in the twentieth century, the growing assertion of the colonized people, and the resultant decline in the legitimacy of western power, the arousal of subaltern voices, the proliferation of new technologies of communication, and the rising consumer culture making a distinction between 'high' and 'low' meaningless. All these factors led many sensitive thinkers in the West to rethink and interrogate the very foundations of modernity.

Thus, post modernists questioned the sanctity of knowledge as an objective quest for truth. For them, science cannot be seen as the master narrative. It has lost its sole claim to truth as science itself is being seen as yet another narrative, a story, and an ideology. Therefore, there is no master truth and no totalizing theory. Instead, in this world of multimodality there are diverse stories and truths. It is a world without consensus, coherence and a meta-theory. In other words, everything is constructed, and there is no natural and permanent truth. Hence all these modern social theory with their totalizing claims, such as, Comte's law of three stages, Durkheim's division of labour leading to organic solidarity, Weber's modernity as widespread rationalization, and Marx's theory of class analysis, lose their significance. And social research becomes merely an act of translation of multiple traditions without any claim for legitimating the grand truth. And as science is being deprived of its validity claim social researchers in the post modern setting become free to play with innumerable sources: narratives, life histories, fictions, popular cinema and music. But then, there are social scientists who do not give their consent to post modernism, even when they see problems with modernity and science. And, in the twenty first century, this debate goes on.

Part II

Philosophical Foundations of Social Research

3

Rationalism

The principal tenet of rationalism or logical thinking is that truth can be best discovered through reason and rational thought. Its basic premise is that the mind may apprehend some truths directly without requiring the medium of the senses. Rationalists assumed that the world is deterministic, and that cause and effect hold for all events, that is to say, *a priori* (from cause to effect) or rational insight is a source of much knowledge. On the other hand, sense experience is seen as being too confusing and tentative. For them, logic and mathematics are classic rational disciplines, as is philosophy. The existence of a rationally deductive objective reality is philosophically linked to the notion of duality exemplified by Descartes, best known as "Cartesian duality." It presupposes the division between the outer objective reality of the phenomenon and the inner subjectivity of the observer. The premise is that for a scientific observation the two must remain separate and that the objective world has a rational reality that is akin to mathematical truth.

The prominent rationalists include Descartes (1596-1650), Spinoza (1632-1677) and Leibniz (1646-1716). Together they formed a part of what came to be known as the rationalist school. Rene Descartes was the most prominent of them all, and regarded as the first modern thinker who has provided a philosophical framework for the natural sciences.

Rene Descartes (1596-1650): Methodological Scepticism

Descartes philosophy developed in the context of Renaissance which rejected religious authority in the quest for scientific and philosophical knowledge. For a long historical time, the advocates of logic had to fight with the domination of religion to establish the supremacy of human reason and mind over the supernatural domain or the will of God. He advocated that society is not a creation of God governed by a divine will but a creation of human beings and an entity that has an objective and changing existence that can be studied from the outside. He projected certain basic premises regarding the truth of social existence. These were in the form of a universal history, holding a basic supposition that all societies are evolved and have gone through various transformations to be what they are today; an idea of progress that things are going towards betterment and the triumph of reason is the ultimate goal of human kind.

Descartes made a number of important contributions to mathematics and physics. Most enduring of his contributions was the foundation of what is now known as analytic geometry. Up to Descartes' time, geometry dealing with lines and shapes, and algebra with numbers appeared as completely different subsets of mathematics. Descartes showed how to translate (almost) all problems in geometry into problems in algebra, by regarding them as questions asking for the length of a line segment, and using a coordinate system to describe the problem. His theory provided the basis for the calculus of Newton and Leibniz, and in this manner for much of modern mathematics.

Descartes attempts to arrive at a fundamental set of principles that one can know as true without any doubt. He questioned, 'What can one know for certain?' In order to answer this, he came forward with a method called *methodological skepticism*. He doubts any idea that can be doubted. He gave the example of dreaming. In a dream, one's senses perceive things that seem real but do not actually exist. He argued that in a similar manner one cannot rely on the data of the senses as necessarily true. Or, he says, perhaps an "evil genius" is present who is a supremely powerful and cunning being, and sets out to try to deceive him from knowing the true nature of reality. Given these possibilities, he asks, what can one know for certain? Initially, he arrived at only a single principle, that is, if I am being deceived, then surely "I" must exist. Most famously, this is known as *Cogito, ergo sum,* which means "I think, therefore I am." In this manner, he concluded that he can be certain that he exists. But the question is in what form? So Descartes proposed that at this point, he would only say that he is thinking thing; thinking is his essence as it is the only thing about him that cannot be doubted.

Descartes demonstrated the limitations of the senses with his *Wax Argument.* He considered a piece of wax and his senses inform him that it has certain characteristics, such as shape, texture, size, colour, smell, and so forth. When he brings the wax towards a flame, these characteristics change completely. However, it seems that it still the same thing; it is still a piece of wax, even though the data of the senses inform him that all of its characteristics are now different. Therefore, in order properly to grasp the nature of the wax, he cannot use the senses and he must use his mind. He concluded, "What thought I had seen with my eyes, I actually grasped solely with the faculty of judgement, which is in my mind."

In this manner Descartes proceeds to construct a system of knowledge, discarding perception as unreliable and instead admitting only deduction as a method. Halfway through the *Method* (published in 1637, entitled in French as *Discours de la Methode*) he also claimed to prove the existence of a benevolent God, who being benevolent, has provided him with a working mind and sensory system, and who cannot desire to deceive him, and thus, finally, he establishes the possibility of acquiring knowledge about the world based on deduction and perception. So it would appear that for Descartes the ultimate certainly emanates from God. This proposition of Descartes did not go too well with the empiricists in England. They were against the pure metaphysical facts. They brought into focus the body and experience as being the source of knowledge. Moreover, Descartes methodology of pure reason and separation of mind and body was a problem which continued to haunt methodologies of the social sciences. In fact, Kant questioned this basic dualism in his book, *Critique of Pure Reason.* Though Kant attempted to remove the dualism he could not fully escape it.

4

Empiricism

Empiricism refers to the view that experience, particularly of the senses, is the only source of knowledge. In other words, the school of philosophers, known as the "empiricists," gave primacy to empirical facts as against the logical knowledge of the rationalists. The basic premise of empiricism is that truth comes only from direct experience, that is to say, words can only be understood if they are connected by their recipient to actual experiences. The word 'empirical' comes from the Greek word *empeiria,* meaning 'experience' and its history goes back to Plato and the Sophists (which has the same root as 'sophisticated'). During eighteenth century, empiricism surfaced as a reaction to rationalist arguments and the events that were transforming the British society influenced the way it took roots in the way Anglo-Saxons perceived social reality. The first of these events was the English civil war in which monarchy and feudalism were challenged. The second was the increasing demand for individual rights and equality among all human beings. The third was unprecedented growth of commerce and science that was fuelled by inventions and discoveries such as Boyle's experiments to understand the basics of gases, Leeuwenhoek's use of the microscope to discover the world of bacteria, and William Harvey's discovery of the circulation of blood. The laws of motion established by Newton (who used Descartes' theory in his calculus) influenced the way the empiricists developed the arguments, which went beyond Descartes' rationalism. The British empiricists rejected the theory of innate ideas and argued that knowledge is based on both sense experience and internal mental experiences, such as emotions and self-reflection, that is, all knowledge comes from experience.

The foremost representatives of the empiricist school were John Locke (1632-1704) and David Hume (1711-1776). John Locke combined the forces of experience and reflection. David Hume's skepticism and questioning on the other hand paved the way for establishing the empiricist tradition in social inquiry. Hume concluded what began with Locke, in laying the foundations for many methodological questions that came up in the philosophy of the sciences.

John Locke (1632-1704): From Sensations to Reflections

For Locke, all ideas come from actual experience. The mind has not innate ideas, but it has innate faculties; it perceives, remembers, and combines the ideas that come to it. The mind desires, deliberates, and wills; and these mental activities are themselves the source of a new class of ideas. Experience is therefore twofold. On the one hand, there are ideas of sensations of seeing, hearing, touching, etc., and on the other there are ideas of reflection, which are thinking, believing, etc. The first ideas are simple where the mind is passive and the second ones of reflection are more complex and active. Such ideas reflect our awareness of our own mental experiences. As for the relation between the idea and the object one experiences, he argues that objects have qualities, which produce an idea in the mind. In his opinion, there were primary and secondary qualities. The primary qualities are produced by the senses such as smell, colour, taste and sound. The secondary qualities are those which refer to bulk, hardness, volume, etc.

In his book, *An Essay Concerning Human Understanding* (1690), Locke offered the outlines of a generic epistemology, and a theory of learning. He was concerned with materials out of which our knowledge is made. He was occupied with discussing how we acquire certain ideas, and how a combination of physical and physiological processes stimulate and work with a large number of mental operations (for example joining, separating, considering, abstracting, generalizing) to produce the ideas of particular sense qualities and many complex notions, such as power, existence, unity. One such complex notion is the idea of self or person. The account of the idea of self, that is, *my* idea of *my* self, emerges out of a discussion of the question, 'Does the soul always think?' That question had been answered in the affirmative by Descartes. For Locke, not only was it empirically false that the soul always thinks, but also that question suggested wrongly that something in me (my soul), not me, thinks. He wrote,

> "I am the agent of my actions and the possessor of my thoughts...all thinking is reflexive; when I think, I am aware that I am thinking, no matter what form that thinking takes (sensing, willing, believing, doubting or remembering). It is the awareness of my act of thinking that also functions in awareness of self. Consciousness appropriate both thoughts and actions" (quoted in Yolton 2004: 589).

The self or person for Locke consists in that set of thoughts and actions which I appropriate and for which I take responsibility through my consciousness. For him, appropriation is a fundamental activity. He writes, "I appropriate my thoughts and actions to form my concept of self." He elaborated, education is also an appropriation of information, but more importantly, of habits of good conduct. Education is a socializing process. It takes place usually within the family, with a tutor (for Locke writes about the education of a gentleman's son). But the account of the socialization process extends to Locke's political writings, *Two Treatises of Government* (1690), where he discusses the family, duties that parents have to their children and to each other (a marriage contract is part of his account of the family), and the rights and duties of citizens in a political society. The appropriation of land, possessions and eventually money by the activities of the person constitutes an early stage in Locke's account of the movement from the state of nature to a civil (political) society (Yolton 2004: 590).

In *Essay*, Locke examined the character and limitations of human knowledge. He pointed out that the mechanical operations of nature remain hidden to us. Careful observation and experimentation may support a reliable set of generalizations about the appearances of the kinds of things we commonly encounter, but we cannot even conceive of their true natures. What we know essentially, according to Locke, is the nominal essence of an idea or thing. Thus, common names for substances are general terms by means of which we classify as we observe them to be. We can agree upon the meaning of such terms even though we remain ignorant of the real essences of the things themselves. Locke held that the extent of our knowledge is quite limited; the most we can hope for is probable knowledge. He extends this argument to the general nature of knowledge and comes up with a deceptively simple notion of knowledge as the perception of agreement or disagreement of ideas. The result of all this is that our knowledge is limited. Thus, for Locke, we can achieve genuine knowledge only when we have clear ideas, and can trace the connection between them enough to perceive their agreement or disagreement. That doesn't happen very often, especially where substances are at issue. Locke's efforts have therefore led to the sobering conclusion that certainty is rarely within our reach and, therefore, we must often be content with probable knowledge or mere opinion.

The methodology for acquiring knowledge recommended by Locke stressed on careful observation and experimentation. Both in the physical science and in learning about ourselves and others, it was the 'plain, historical method,' that is, experience and observation, that holds the promise of accurate knowledge, or sound probability knowledge was not limited to demonstrative, deductive processes. Truth claims were always open to revision through further reports and observations. These concepts of knowledge and the experiential method were extended by Locke to what was later termed (for example by Hume) 'the science of man' or 'of human nature'. His detailed attention to his own thought processes enabled him to map the wide variety of mental operations and to begin the development of a cognitive psychology. His interest in children, throughout his life, led to observations and descriptions of their behaviour. He had many friends who had children, and lived for several years on different occasions with families who had several young children. The *Essay* uses some of these observations as the basis for a brief genetic learning theory, and his *Some Thoughts Concerning Education* (1693) contains many remarks and recommendations for raising children based upon his first-hand experience with children in their natural environment (Yolton 2004: 590).

Locke's interest in children is reflected not only in his pedagogical work, *Some Thoughts Concerning Education* (1693), but in many passages of the *Essay* where he traced the development of awareness in children. The oft-quoted metaphor used by Locke to characterize the mind as a blank tablet should not blind us to the fact that the Lockean mind comes equipped with faculties, that the child has specific 'tempers' or character traits which the educator must learn to work with. Human nature for Locke has basic self-preserving tendencies to avoid pain and seek pleasure. These tendencies were even called by Locke 'innate practical principles.' The innate claim that his psychology rejected was for truths (moral and intellectual) and specific ideational contents (Ibid.: 589).

Locke's social and political theory grew out of his reading and, more importantly, out of these habits of observing people in daily life. In his travels in France and Holland, he often recorded details of activities and practices, religious, academic and ordinary. Where direct observation was not possible, he used the new travel literature for reports on other societies, other customs and habits. He had his own biases and preference, to be sure, but with his dedication to reason and rationality, he seldom allowed emotions to effect his observation or his conclusions. He was an articulate representative of the Royal Society's attitudes in the sciences, including what we know as the social sciences.

The political society, as the prepolitical state of nature, is grounded in law and order; order is respect and responsibility to each other and ultimately to God whose law of nature prescribes these duties. Locke's law of nature is a Christianized version of that tradition. The individual laws that he cites on occasion prescribe and proscribe the action sanctioned or denied by the liberal religion of his day. These laws differed little in content from those innate moral truths Locke attacked; it was not the truths he rejects, only the claim that they were innate. Locke's society is fairly slanted in favour of the individual; preservation of the person, privacy of property, tacit assent and the right of dissent. At the same time, the pressures towards conformity and the force of majority opinion are also strong. He believed that there were no divine rights for monarchs to rule, and that human beings are free and in this condition all human beings are equal. The structure of his civil society, with its checks and balances, its separation of powers, its grounding on the law of nature, is designed to achieve a balance between the rights and needs of the individual and the need for security and order. His views on toleration (which were expressed in a series of tracts), while directed mainly against religious intoleration, match well with his insistence that government does not have the right to prescribe rites, rituals, dress and other practices in religion. Locke's toleration did not, however, extend to unbelief, to atheism (Kuper 2004:590).

Locke influenced the way his contemporaries viewed the process of human understanding. Many of them disagreed with his ideas. His main critique came from George Berkeley (1685-1753) who wrote two books, *Treatises Concerning the Principles of Human knowledge* (1710) , and *Three Dialogues between Hylas and Philonous* (1734) in his reply to the views of John Locke. Quite contrary to Locke's theories that the fundamental essence of the world was matter; and mind was only a passive instrument, George Berkeley placed mind first and asserted that things exist only when they are perceived by a mind. Locke has his supporters too. One of them was the Scottish philosopher, David Hume, who applied Locke's ideas in a logical manner and argued that all thought is built up from simple and separate impressions. Hume takes another step and reduces one's expectations of certainty of knowledge by being skeptic to begin with.

David Hume (1711-1776): Belief as a Habit

As an empiricist, David Hume put forward that 'as human beings do in fact live and function in the physical world, we should try to observe how they do so.' According to Hume, the proper goal of philosophy is simply to explain why we believe what we do. In *A Treatise of Human Nature* (1739-1740), his analysis of human belief begins with a careful distinction among our mental contents of impressions, which are the direct, vivid, and forceful products of immediate experience. For him, ideas are mere copies of these original impressions. For example, 'the colour of the tree at which I am now looking is an impression, while my memory of the colour of my mother's hair is merely an idea.' Hume supposed, since each idea must be derived from an antecedent impression, it always makes sense to inquire into the origins of the idea by asking from which impressions it is derived.

Hume elaborated that the apparent connection of one idea to another is invariably the result of an association that we manufacture ourselves. We use our mental operations to link ideas to each other in one of three ways: resemblance, contiguity, or cause and effect. Experience provides us with both the ideas themselves and our awareness of their associations. All human beliefs result from repeated applications of these simple associations. For him, such beliefs can reach beyond the content of present sense-impressions and memory, by appealing to presumed connections of cause and effect. But since each idea is distinct and separable from every other, there is no self-evident relation. These connections can only be derived from our experience of similar cases. He argued that causal reasoning can never be justified rationally. In order to learn, we must suppose that our past experiences bear some relevance to present and future cases. Although, we do indeed believe that the future will be like the past, the truth of that belief is not self-evident. In fact, it is always possible for nature to change, so inferences from past to future are never rationally certain. Thus, in Hume's view, all beliefs as a matter of fact are fundamentally non-rational.

To justify, Hume's favourite example about our belief is that 'the sun will rise tomorrow.' Clearly, this is a matter of fact; it rests on our conviction that each sunrise is an effect caused by the rotation of the earth. But our belief in that causal relation is based on past observations, and our confidence that it will continue tomorrow cannot be justified by reference to the past. So we have no rational basis for believing that the sun will rise tomorrow. Yet we do believe it.

In *The Enquiries Concerning Human Understanding* (1748), Hume postulated that skepticism quite properly forbids us to speculate beyond the content of our present experience and memory, yet we find it entirely natural to believe much more than that. He held that these unjustifiable beliefs can be explained by reference to custom or habit, that is, how we learn from experience. So he asserted that belief is a matter of habit. He wrote;

> "When I observe the constant conjunction of events in my experience, I grow accustomed to associating them with each other. Although many past cases of sunrise do not guarantee the future of nature, my experience of them does get me used to the idea and produces in me an expectation that the sun will rise again tomorrow. I cannot prove that it will, but I feel that it must."

He pointed out that the association of ideas is a powerful natural process in which separate ideas come to be joined together in the mind. He argued, 'of course they can be associated with each other by rational means, as they are in the relations of ideas that constitute mathematical knowledge. But even where this is possible, reason is a slow and inefficient guide, while the habits acquired by much repetition can produce powerful conviction that is independent of reason.' For Hume, our beliefs in matters of fact arise from sentiment rather than from reason; and imagination and belief differ only in the degree of conviction with which their objects are anticipated. Although this positive answer may seem disappointing, Hume maintained that custom or habit is the guide of life and the foundation of all natural sciences.

In fact, Hume supposed that our belief in the reality of an external world is entirely non-rational. It cannot be supported either as a relation of ideas or even as a matter of fact. Although it is utterly unjustifiable, however, belief in the external world is natural and unavoidable. We are in the habit of supposing that our ideas have external referents, even though we can have no real evidence for doing so. According to Hume, knowledge of pure mathematics is secure because its rests only on the relations of ideas, without presuming anything about the world. Experimental observations (conducted without any assumption of the existence of material objects) permit us to use our experience in forming useful habits. Any other epistemological effort, especially if it involves the pretence of achieving useful abstract knowledge, is meaningless and unreliable. The most reasonable position, Hume held, is a "mitigated" skepticism that humbly accepts the limitations of human knowledge while pursuing the legitimate aims of mathematics and the sciences. In our non-philosophical moments, of course, we will be thrown back upon the natural beliefs of everyday life, no matter how lacking in rational. Hume thought that a human being is a bundle of different perceptions and in that sense has no fixed identity. He criticised the idea that everything has a cause. In fact, he doubted everything that we assume on the basis of our common sense and also on the basis of scientific knowledge. Philosophers have found it hard to answer his penetrating doubts. Hume influenced philosophical debates about principles of knowledge.

Thus, what John Locke said about the ways of acquiring knowledge, that is, 'our ideas about things come out of our experience of sensations and reflections,' Hume takes it further by concluding that a lot of what we think of as certainties was only habits. Hume is generally regarded as one of the most important philosopher ever to write in English. His major philosophical works remained widely and deeply influential, despite being denounced by many of his contemporaries as works of skepticism and atheism. Hume's influence was evident in the moral philosophy and economic writings of his close friend Adam Smith, and "caused the scales to fall" from Jeremy Bentham's eyes. Charles Darwin counted Hume as a central influence. Hume has been described as awakening Kant from his "dogmatic slumber;" it is partly as a reacting to Hume that Kant attempted a theory of knowledge. He wanted to rise above the skepticism of Hume to look for certainties, yet, he was not in favour of the pure rationalism of Descartes. Immanuel Kant took rationality of the human mind to a transcendental level and this attempt put him in the category of idealists.

5

Idealism

Idealism refers to system of thought in which the object of external perception is held to be consists of ideas. It holds that the mind plays a key role in the constitution of the world as it is experienced. In the history of thought we discern different forms and applications of idealism. Plato thought that all properties and objects we could think of must have some such independent existence. Confusingly, this kind of idealism was once termed "realism." Hegel (1770-1831) thought that history must be rational in something significantly like the way science is. It denotes the belief that abstract or mental entities have some sort of reality "independent" of the world. Its most radical form has been rejected because it was equivalent to solipsism, that is, all reality is nothing but the activities of one's own mind and that in reality nothing exists but one's own self. Idealists generally recognise the existence of the external or natural world and do not claim that it can be reduced to the mere process of thinking. They believe that the mind is active and capable of producing and sustaining modes of being that would not have existed otherwise, such as law, religion, art and mathematics. In other words, ideas have objective existence and matter as an object of perception has real existence. In this sense, idealism is a theory that posits the primacy of spirit, mind, or language over matter. It claimed that thought has a crucial role in making the world the way it is, that is to say, thought and the world are made for one another, or, they make one another.

George Berkeley (1685-1753)

The eighteenth century Irish philosopher George Berkeley is closely identified with the idealist philosophy. He believed that all aspects of everything of which we are conscious are actually reducible to the ideas present in the mind. For example, the idea of a chair or a cow already exists in our minds; therefore, we recognise the chair or the cow when we find it. Thus the observer does not conjure the external objects (chair or cow) into existence. In fact, Berkeley held that the true ideas of the external objects are caused directly by God.

Immanuel Kant (1724-1804): *A Priori* Categories

The eighteenth century German philosopher, Immanuel Kant carried forward the idealist tradition through his critical inquiry into the limits of possible knowledge. Kant held that the mind forces the world we perceive to take the shape of space-and-time. He tried to move beyond the traditional dichotomy between rationalism and empiricism. The rationalist had faith in that we can understand the world by careful use of reason; this guarantees the undoubtability of our knowledge but left serious questions about its practical content. The empiricist, on the other hand, had argued that all of our knowledge must be firmly grounded in experience; practical content was thus secured, but it turned out that we could be certain of very little. For Kant, both approaches had failed because they were premised on the same mistaken assumption.

Kant was born in Konigsberg, Germany. He rarely ever left the small town that he lived in. He grew in the background of pious religious upbringing. Though he did not attend Church in his later years he kept his German Puritanical upbringing intact. Yet, he could not isolate himself from the skeptical current of that time. The men whom he later aimed to refute, and most of all Hume, influenced Kant. Kant's life "passed like the most regular of regular verbs, rising, coffee-drinking, writing, lecturing, dining, and walking". During these quiet years he wrote on many things, physical as well as metaphysical. He wrote about planets, earth, and volcanoes and on anthropology and even on pedagogy (Durant 1961: 261-262). He had great faith in moral freedom, in human beings' ability to choose what is right.

In his book, *The Critique of Pure Reason* (1781), Kant explained his ideas about the foundations of our knowledge of the physical world. Instead of criticizing pure reason, rather he highlighted its limitations. In fact, he tried to exalt pure reason to transcendental level without the corrupting elements of the senses. He is not totally against the role that the senses play nor is he disavowing reason. What he does is to combine both empiricist and rationalist elements. For that, he distinguished between where our knowledge originates and what kind of knowledge it is. He explained that in an analytical proposition, the predicate is contained in the subject. For example, the cricket balls are round. In a synthetic proposition, the subject and predicate are independent of each other. To explain further, Kant maintained that *a priori* knowledge comes purely from reasoning independent of experience. For example 4+4=8 is an example of *a priori* knowledge. A *posteriori* knowledge is based on sensory experience. For example, the statement, 'The bird is sitting on the tree,' is based on sensory experience.

Furthermore, Kant went on to explain exactly how the thought process worked. According to him we have some intuitive categories such as space and time, which are absolute and independent of and preceding sense impressions. On the question of Berkeley's problem of whether we will ever know the reality or the essence of objects, Kant has no problem with the existence of objects. "The mere existence of my own consciousness proves the existence of objects outside of me" (quoted in Osborne 1991: 103). But Kant sets limits to knowledge and distinguishes between *phenomena* and *noumena*. According to Kant, it is vital always to distinguish between the distinct realms of *phenomena* and *noumena*. All of our synthetic *a priori* judgements apply only to the realm of phenomena. While *phenomena* are the appearances, which constitute our experience; *noumena* are the things themselves, which constitute reality, or what he calls *ding-and-sich* (the thing in itself). Since the *thing in itself* would by definition be entirely independent of our experience of it, we are utterly ignorant of the noumenal realm.

In Kant's view, the most fundamental laws of nature, like the truths of mathematics, are knowable precisely because they make no effort to describe the world as it really is but rather prescribe the structure of the world as we experience it. By applying the pure forms of sensible intuition and the pure concepts of the understanding, we achieve a systematic view of the phenomenal realm but learn nothing of the noumenal realm. Mathematics and the sciences are certainly true of the *phenomena*; only metaphysics claims to instruct us about the *noumena* which according to Kant are beyond our realm of knowledge.

6

Positivism

Positivism emerged out tremendous optimism centred on the cognitive power of science. Modern social science evolved at a specific juncture of European history when the entire social landscape altered because of the scientific revolution, the Enlightenment and the French revolution. It was indeed a new age, and social science as a formal-academic discipline was trying to make sense of it. As a method of social research, it sought to give immense cognitive prestige to the discipline engaged in social enquiry and explanations, and tried to convince its adherents that the scientific methodological principles of empirical observation, deductive reasoning, and formulation of laws or universal generalizations could be followed in the sociological study.

The origin of positivism could be traced back to the first half of the nineteenth century in France. In the post-revolutionary period, there was a significant change in the domain of knowledge. The separation of science and philosophy became inevitable; new scientific journals started appearing, and a close link between science and industry was established. It was felt that there was a single scientific method applicable to all fields of study. Saint Simon (1760-1825) articulated this aspiration rather sharply and therefore, pleaded strongly for extending the scientific outlook from the physical sciences to the study of human beings. A scientist, he felt, is one who predicts, and it is this power of prediction that gives him the power. Indeed, this close affinity with science gave birth to positivism, that is to say, an urge to create some kind of a "social physics."

Auguste Comte (1798-1857): Inductive Positivism

Like Saint Simon, Comte too was influenced by the revolutionary transformation. In a way, he witnessed the contradiction between the two social forces: theological/military and scientific/industrial. Like a visionary, he felt that this contradiction could be resolved only by the triumph of the scientific/industrial society. Scientists, as he saw all around, were replacing theologians as the "moral guardians" of the new social order and industrialists were replacing the warriors. Not solely that. Comte too shared the Enlightenment assertion that it was possible for science to grasp the workings of the world. He believed that positivist or scientific knowledge was the inevitable outcome of the progressive growth of the individual mind as well as the historical development of human knowledge. From 1771 to 1823 Comte and Saint Simon collaborated so closely that it was almost impossible to distinguish the contributions of the two. It was at this juncture that they spoke of social physics and the need to discover natural and immutable laws of progress which are as necessary as the law of gravity. But then they separated, and eventually Comte emerged as an independent scholar. It was during 1830-1842 that he published six volumes of *Course of Positive Philosophy*, and during 1851-1854, he published four volumes of *System of Positive Politics*.

Comte's works reflect his engagement with the methodology of scientific thought. He argued, "Like scientists who studied the natural world and discovered the nature of laws determining the behaviour of matter in the physical world, it was possible to discover the laws which determined the behaviour of people in the social world." In his book, *Course of Positive Philosophy*, he postulated that laws governing the behaviour of people in the social world could be discovered through the development of a positive philosophy of human social development. In other words, he opined that social scientists could use the methodology and insight of the natural sciences as the model for the development of the science of society. He said,

> "In the...positive state, the mind has given over the vain search after the Absolute notions, the origin and destination of the universe, and the causes of phenomena, applies itself to the study of their laws ...their invariable relations of succession and resemblance. Reasoning and observation, duly combined, are the

> means to this knowledge. What we now understand when we speak of an explanation of facts is simply establishment of a connection between single phenomena and some general facts, the number of which diminishes with the progress of science."

In Comte's view, the aim of science was the explanation of how things related to one another in terms of invariable and universal laws. In this sense, observable phenomena are the main ingredients of positive science, which aims to establish law-like relations between phenomena through gathering of factual knowledge which is carried out through observation, experimentation, comparison and prediction. The idea is that after discovering a wide range of laws, it would be possible to explain the laws in terms of their relationship to each other.

For Comte, science means the progressive discovery of laws and their interrelationships so that science could one day propound a general law from which all other laws emanate. He assumed that the social world was as regular and objective as was the natural world. For him, social laws governed the social world just as natural laws governed the natural world. Comte, thus, considered the methodology of the natural sciences the ideal way to discover laws governing the social world and he advocated the development of a new positive outlook, based on the methodology of the natural sciences. He divided the general laws into the two categories: first, the laws of co-existence or social static and second, the laws of succession or social dynamics. The former governed the relationship between different parts of society and as such they determined the functions and interrelationship between the various parts. The latter governed social change and required an exploration of the way the nature and function of social institutions changed over time.

As evident from his assumptions and observation, Comte followed the methodology of the nineteenth century natural sciences for positing the principles of natural sciences to the study of human social development. His first assumption was that societies pass through a process of evolution and their stages of development are from the simple to the complex. In this sense, societies gradually become more complex and institutionally differentiated, performing specific functions. His second assumption is based on the fact that in order to integrate the incremental differences in societies the mechanisms leading to social integration need to involve one or the other form of mutual dependence. He concluded that evolution is both a natural and demonstrable fact and it is governed by Laws of Development. He argued that the task of social researchers was to discover the Laws of Development by systematic observation; collection of data or facts; and development of theories to explain the facts. The logic of Comte's ideas is called *inductivism* or *inductive positivism*. This is also referred to as the nineteenth century positivism to differentiate it from positivism, as a methodology developed in the twentieth century which was quite different from Comte's conception.

According to Comte, 'all phenomena are subject to invariable natural laws; in so far as human phenomena are concerned, the fundamental laws are the laws concerning the human beings' intellectual history, the evolution of the way of thinking of human beings about themselves and the world around them.' Based on the reasoning of his inductive positivism, he gave three stages of evolution of human society: the age of religion, that is, *the theological or fictitious state*; the age of metaphysics, that is, *the metaphysical or abstract state*; and the age of reason, that is, *the scientific or positive state*. He argued that this law of the three stages, like the law of gravity, had been at work since the beginning of the human being's life on earth; each branch of our knowledge has passed successively through three different theoretical conditions. In the *theological state*, the mind supposes all phenomena to be produced by the immediate action of supernatural beings, that is, a state in which the mind explains phenomena or mundane occurrences by ascribing them to the unfathomable gods. The fact is that without some guide one cannot begin to make systematic observations. And sciences in their infancy could not escape the questions relating to the essences of phenomena and their ultimate origins to which theological answers are most appropriate. In the *metaphysical state*, the mind supposes abstract forces, veritable entities, inherent in all beings, that is, a state in which abstract forces, powers and essences, rather than spiritual forces, are considered responsible for worldly affairs. And finally, as Comte argued, there was a *positive or scientific state* in which we abandon the search for ultimate origins, purposes, or abstract forces, and become more concrete and focused: we observe the relations between phenomena, and arrive at laws because the aim of positive philosophies to consider all phenomena as subject to invariable natural laws. In other words, the mind has given over the vain search after Absolute notions, the origin and destination of the universe and the causes of phenomena, and applies itself to the study of their laws, that is, their invariable relations of succession and resemblance. Various disciplines like physics and biology had passed through the theological and the metaphysical stages and had now become scientific.

Comte pointed out that not all branches of knowledge reach the positive stage simultaneously. He elaborated, the 'lower' sciences, like astronomy, mechanics, and chemistry develop fast. These are lower sciences because these are less complex, less dependent on the other sciences, and their distance from human affairs is far greater. But human science, being more complex, and more near to everyday life, would reach the positive stage quite late. Comte was, however, hopeful that even for human science the time had finally arrived. It could now project itself as a positive science, analyze social phenomena, and discover the laws governing the relations among them. He clarified that there are two kinds of sciences, namely, *analytic* and *synthetic*. Physics and chemistry can be said to be *analytic* because they establish laws among isolated phenomena. Biology is *synthetic* because it is impossible to explain an organ apart from the living creature as a whole. Likewise, according to Comte, human science is synthetic because everything, be it religion or state, has to be studied in the context of the entire society. He stated, "There is no free will in mathematics and physics." Likewise, Comte argued, there is no free will in human science.

Thus, Comte was a great proponent of science. He believed in the essential the Enlightenment notion of progress and in the arrival of the new age of scientific objectivity. Also, Comte was a great moralist. He was deeply concerned about social order and its moral foundation. In fact, he sought to use positivist human science to reconstruct his society. No wonder, positivist human science, for him, would act like a religion, of course a secular religion for humankind. That's why an eminent scholar has commented "positivist human science for Comte is simply medievalism minus Christianity" (Nisbet 1967: 58). In the post revolution period, the French society was confronting with new problems which, as Comte put forward, were quite disturbing. For instance, he could not give his consent to the prevalent "anarchy" leading to exaggerated individualism. It was, for him, a disease of modern civilization. Nor did he give his consent to those who pleaded for divorce rights. His anxiety was that it would lead to the breakdown of the centrality of the family; it would also weaken the community. This moral crisis, or the crisis of order, was something that must be resolved. And it was his conviction that the new positivist sociological knowledge could fulfill the void and serve the therapeutic function of religion.

Emile Durkheim (1858-1917): Meaning of Social Fact

In *The Rules of Sociological Method*, published in 1895, Durkheim consolidated and elaborated positivist human science. The subject matter of human science, he emphasized, is the domain of social facts that cannot be comprehended by any other discipline. He defined, "A social fact is every way of acting, fixed or not, capable of exercising on the individual an external constraint; or again, every way of acting which is general throughout a given society, while at the same time existing in its own right independent of its individual manifestations" (1964: 13). He elaborated, "their source is not in the individual, their substratum can be no other than society, either the political society as a whole or someone of the partial groups it includes, such as religious denominations, political, literary, and occupational associations" (1964: 3). To clarify, he stated, walking barefoot inside the temple is a fact that exists out there as a thing. It has an independent force that transcends your own will. If you disobey the practice, you would be forced, coerced, isolated or ridiculed. Well, you may argue that it is you who have chosen to walk barefoot inside the temple complex. But that is because you have internalized the prevalent practice so well that it looks almost natural and spontaneous. The reason is that, because of habit, socialization and internalization, we tend to experience social facts as natural and spontaneous. Such facts are called social facts.

Durkheim pointed out three distinctive features of social facts. First, social facts exist outside you. He explained,

> "When I fulfill my obligations as brother, husband, or citizen, when I execute my contracts, I perform duties which are defined, externally to myself, and my acts, in law and in custom. Even if they conform to my sentiments and I feel their reality subjectively,

> such reality is still objective, for I did not create them; I merely inherited through my education. Imagine a tree that you are seeing from your window. It has a reality of its own. Even if you close your eyes and refuse to see it, the tree exists as it is" (1964: 1).

As Durkheim put it, "here are ways of acting, thinking, and feeling that present the noteworthy property of existing outside the individual consciousness" (1964: 2). The currency you use in your economic exchange, the language you speak in the process of communication, the rituals you celebrate as a member of a religious community, all these are social facts. Their existence does not depend on your or my will. Second, social facts are endowed with coercive power. He stated, "if I do not submit to the conventions of my society, if in my dress I do not conform to the customs observed in my country and in my class, the ridicule I provoke, the social isolation in which I am kept, produce, although in an attenuated form, the same effects as a punishment in the strict sense of the word" (1964: 2-3). Third, social facts as things need to be distinguished from their individual manifestations. In fact, Durkheim held that social facts "acquire a body, a tangible form, and constitute a reality in their own right, quite distinct from the individual facts which produce it". For example, codified legal and moral rules, or articles of faith wherein religious groups condense their beliefs; none of these can be found entirely reproduced in the applications made of them by individuals. Yet, sociologically it is important to categorize their tangible, crystallized aspects as social facts, not their individual manifestations.

Durkheim prescribed the "rules" for studying social facts. One such rule which has often been talked about is that it is absolutely necessary to observe social facts as things. He explained,

> "Social facts.... qualify as things. Law is embodied in codes; the currents of daily life are recorded in statistical figures and historical monuments; fashions are preserved in costumes; and taste in works of art. By their very nature they tend towards an independent existence outside the individual consciousness, which they dominate. In order to disclose their characters as things, it is unnecessary to manipulate them ingeniously" (1964: 30).

He continued, 'a thing is a thing because its facticity cannot be altered even if you and I want it. It is in this sense that external objects like a tree, a table and a chair exist as things. If you wish to observe a thing as it is, you should not confuse it with your own ideas and sentiments. A tree needs to be seen as a tree, even if you hate trees.' In other words, almost like Francis Bacon, Durkheim would argue that our ideas and sentiments or "idols" should not prevent us from seeing a thing as it is. A social researcher must follow this fundamental lesson of scientific objectivity. Take, for instance, marriage as a social fact. As an individual, you may not like the institution of marriage. But when as a social researcher you plan to study marriage as a social fact, retain your objectivity, separate your own likes and dislikes from facts, and see it as a thing codified in marriage laws, religious traditions and social customs. In other words, it is like separating the knower from the known facts from values. It is similar to the way a physicist studies the behaviour of atoms, or a geologist studies the formation of mountains.

Likewise, Durkheim recalled Rene Descartes, and reminded us of the need for overcoming all presuppositions. For Durkheim, it is like overcoming "inferior" faculties like emotions, sentiments and feelings. Only then is it possible for social researcher 'to emancipate himself from the fallacious ideas that dominate the mind of the layman (1964: 32). No wonder, he pleaded strongly for a scientific vocabulary in the discipline. Social researchers must avoid the indeterminacy of common sense language, and they should have clarity about the specificity of the concept. He said, "The subject matter of every sociological study should comprise a group of phenomena defined in advance by certain common external characteristics, and all phenomena so defined should be included within this group" (1964: 35). It is equally important to avoid all sorts of vagueness while studying/observing an object. The physicist substitutes for the vague impressions of temperature and electricity by the visual representations of the thermometer and the electrometer. Likewise, when a sociologist studies social facts, she/he should not be carried away by their individual manifestations. Instead, it is important to find their expression in tangible and crystallized forms; for example, in legal codes, moral regulations, popular proverbs, statistical figures and religious conventions.

Durkheim argued that "a whole is not identical with the sum of its parts" (1964: 102). It acquires an independent character that is qualitatively different from those of its component parts. Society is, therefore, not identical with the sum of individuals. It is, of course, true that without individuals there is no society. But society transcends the individual. While explaining social facts, it is important to understand the supremacy of the collective over the individual. He clarified,

> "The group thinks, feels and acts quite differently from the way in which its members would were they isolated. If, then, we begin with the individual, we shall be able to understand nothing of what takes place in the group. In a word, there is between psychology and sociology the same break in continuity as between biology and the physiochemical sciences. Consequently every time that a social phenomenon is directly explained by a psychological phenomenon, we could be sure that the explanation is false" (1964: 104).

In fact, as Durkheim categorically stated, 'the determining cause of a social fact should be sought among the social facts preceding it and not among the states of individual consciousness' (1964: 110). Likewise, the function of a social fact needs to be seen in its relation to some social end. Take, for instance, punishment as a social fact. For Durkheim, its cause is the intensity of the collective sentiments that the crime offends. Likewise, its function is to maintain these very sentiments at the same degree of intensity. No wonder, for him, when the teacher punishes the child its function is not to cause physical suffering to the concerned child but to restore the sanctity of moral order in the classroom. To explain a social phenomenon, as Durkheim argued, is to find its cause as well as its function. And both cause and function are essentially social, not to be reduced to the individual psyche.

Moreover, Durkheim was deeply concerned about the moral foundation of society, its stability and order. Possibly modern/ industrial societies, and their implicit differentiation, specialization and division of labour made him confront a new problem. Gone are the days of simple societies characterized by 'mechanical solidarity'. But then, can modern societies survive merely through egotistic individualism and selfish interests? No wonder, he evolved a strong critique of utilitarianism and its celebration of the atomized individual trying to maximize one's pleasure. Instead, Durkheim continued to retain his belief in the moral supremacy of the collective, and he saw that the increasing differentiation in a modern society, paradoxically, would lead to more and more mutual dependence and create 'organic solidarity'.

Thus, in both Auguste Comte and Emile Durkheim, it seems that positivism is both an assertion of science as well as a quest for order and stability. It was this consistent search for the basis of moral order that led him to explore the domain of religion and of the sacred, and school and moral education. In a way, they endeavour to reconcile positivist sociological study with social order and stability. And, to achieve this, they put forward that the principle of causality can be applied to social phenomena, that is, 'to assume the exacting character befitting every science.' Durkheim concluded, 'social facts are external and coercive; it should be treated as things' to be studied through concrete expression in legal codes, religious expressions, proverbs, customs etc.

CRITIQUES OF POSITIVISM

Positivism emerged at a time when sociological study was trying to establish itself as a science. In order to provide a 'scientific status' to itself, that is to say, the urge to reduce qualitative human experiences into quantified statistical figures, the search for precision, objectivity, causality and value neutrality were accepted as method culminating into the mathematization of social phenomena. But then, with the passage of time, with new experiences leading to disillusionment with the so called 'neutrality' of science, and with new sensitivity to reflexivity and creativity, positivism has lost much of its appeal. The critiques alleged, 'positivism undermines the creativity, reflexivity and agency of social actors. Society consists of self-reflexive agents who think, argue, contest, and through their practices and actions transform the world.'

Alvin Gouldner (1920-1980): Methodological Monism

Gouldner pleaded against the methodological dualism implicit in positivism. This dualism, according to him, separates the knower from the known, subject from object, and fact from value. He argued, 'this cold objectivity is essentially an expression of alienation, that is, the alienation of the sociologist from his/her own self. It is like looking at sociological knowledge as just a piece of amoral technique. In *The Coming Crisis of Western Sociology,* he wrote,

> "Methodological dualism is based upon a fear; but this is a fear not so much of those being studied as of the sociologist's own self. Methodological dualism is, at bottom, concerned to constitute a strategy for coping with the feared vulnerability of the scholar's self. It strives to free him from disgust, pity, anger, from egoism or moral outrage, from his passions and interest, on the supposition that it is a bloodless and disembodied mind that works best. It also seeks to insulate the scholar from the values and interests of his other roles and commitments, on the dubious assumption that these can be anything but blinders. It assumes that feeling is the blood enemy of intelligence, and that there can be an unfeeling, unsentimental knower" (1970: 496).

Instead, he favoured *methodological monism*, that is, 'the separation between the knower and the known must be overcome, because you cannot know others without knowing yourself.' Knowing is not an impersonal effort but 'a personalized effort by whole, embodied men' (1970: 493). Reflexive sociology invites methodological monism, and, therefore, alters the very meaning of knowledge. It does not remain merely a piece of information. Instead, it becomes awareness. It generates self-awareness and new sensitivity. Unlike positivist sociology in which you can remain 'neutral' and 'apolitical', reflexive sociology demands your moral commitment and ethical engagement. You cannot separate your life from your work' (1970: 493). He wrote,

> "Reflexive sociology, then, is not characterized by what it studies. It is distinguished neither by the persons and the problems studied nor even by the techniques and instruments used in studying them. It is characterized, rather, by a relationship it establishes between being a sociologist and being a person, between the role and the man performing it. Reflexive sociology embodies a critique of the conventional conception of segregated scholarly roles and has a vision of an alternative. It aims at transforming the sociologist's relation to his work" (1970: 495).

Hence, what is applicable in the domain of nature is not necessarily applicable in the domain of human society, that is, society cannot be subject to abstract/universal generalizations.

Anthony Giddens: Theory of Structuration

Giddens is categorical about the fact that nature and human society are two different realms of enquiry. Nature is not a human production, but society is being perpetually created, renewed and altered by human agents. That is why there are limits to natural science methodology in sociological research. In *New Rules of Sociological Method* (1976), he analyzed the intellectual trajectory of the discipline, and negotiated with interpretative traditions, and reflexed on a set of new rules. It does offer an alternative to positivistic/scientific sociology. He began his intellectual conversation with phenomenological/ethno methodological traditions, the way these 'interpretative' sociological explanations seek to understand meanings, that is, the meanings that conscious human actors attach to the world, and construct their knowledge of the everyday world they live in. He argues, in sociology 'those who still wait for a Newton are not only waiting for a train that won't arrive, they're in the wrong station altogether' (1976: 13).

Giddens' theory of structuration is based on the premise that 'social life is more than random individual acts, but is not merely determined by social forces.' It is not merely a mass of 'micro-level activity,' but on the other hand, one cannot study it by only looking for macro-level explanations.' He defined structuration as 'the process by way of which social structures are formed; as in much practical-theoretical work, this concept aims to unify action-oriented and structure.' Instead, he argued, 'human agency and social structure are in a relationship with each other, and it is the repetition of the acts of individual agents, which reproduces the structure. This means that there is a social structure, that is, traditions, institutions, moral codes, and established ways of doing things; but it also means that these can be changed when people start to ignore them, replace them, or reproduce them differently.' He put forward that there are possibilities in these traditions 'to see beyond,' because 'the meaning you and I attach to the world has to be situated in a social context, and asymmetrical resources and capabilities often characterize this context.' To explain, he cited a classroom situation as an example. Imagine yourself as a student in the classroom. It is, of course, true that you are not a puppet silently performing the prescribed 'role'. Instead, you are a creative agent attaching meanings, and creating an inter-subjective world called the classroom. But, then, there is a problem. Your agency/freedom is not unlimited. Because differential/unequal resources might characterize the classroom: teacher versus student. Even a simple site like the classroom is, in fact, a site of conflict and contestation. Therefore, he put forward that interpretative sociology alone is not sufficient; it is equally important to be aware of the complex relationship between the agency and structure. He added, 'although society is a skilled performance, the creativity of the social actor, is not unlimited since all of us, irrespective of our creativity, are historically located social actors, working under certain conditions. It is in this context that we ought to be aware of the limits/constraints provided by the social structure.' But then, what is interesting about Giddens is that he is talking about the duality of structure. 'Structure must not be conceptualized as simply placing constraints upon human agency, but as enabling' (1976: 161).

To substantiate, Giddens cited an example of speaking a language. He pointed out that 'no matter how creative you are, you cannot speak whatever you wish. You have to follow the grammar: a set of rules. But then, it is not just an experience of constraint. Language also enables you to speak.' Moreover, 'a living language is not static; through their linguistic expressions and practices people make changes in the structure of the language.' This is what he regarded as the process of structuration. For him, 'to enquire into the structuration of social practices is to seek to explain how it comes about that structures are constituted through action and, reciprocally, how action is constituted structurally'. In a way, the process of structuration enables him to overcome the duality of structure and agency. He argued, 'yes, you cannot imagine yourself without the "rules" that the structure provides. But at the same time, you are not a puppet. You can innovate, experiment, and alter the structure' (Ibid.).

Therefore, this critical/creative engagement with methodological issues led Giddens to provide a set of rules. First, sociological inquiry is not concerned with a "pre-given" universe of objects. Instead, it deals with a world that is constituted or provided by the active doings of subjects. It is in this sense that 'the production and reproduction of society has to be treated as a skilled performance on the part of its members'. He asserted that a social researcher cannot escape the language that lay actors use to make sense of their world. It is precisely for this reason that meaningful sociological research requires immersion in the form of life which the social researcher seeks to study. He clarified, "Immersion does not, however, mean that the sociologist has to become a 'full member' of the community. This only means the ability to participate in it as an ensemble of practices" (1976: 160). Further, he stated, sociological concepts are based on double hermeneutic. The reason is that social actors themselves have already interpreted society as being a skilled performance, and hence the social researchers further reinterpret it within their theoretical schemes mediating ordinary and technical language.

The Frankfurt School Marxism

In the mid-twentieth century, the critique of positivism came rather sharply from the adherents of the Frankfurt School Marxism, or critical theorists, namely, Adorno, Horkheimer, Marcuse, etc. They asserted that science has lost its emancipatory power. Instead, they argued, 'science itself has become an integral component of the establishment.' In fact, the experience of war, large-scale violence, the growth of fascism, the spread of the "culture industry," and the emergence of the 'authoritarian personality,' that is to say, "the darkness of the twentieth century" led these thinkers to speak of the 'dialectic of enlightenment.' The central thrust of their argument was that positivist science was nothing but a form of instrumental rationality leading to domination and manipulation of human and natural resources. They critiqued this instrumental rationality, and pleaded for a more critical, reflexive, qualitative and emancipatory social science. They argued that that the so-called "ethical neutrality" of positivism reduces it to a mere technique, separated from moral/political issues. And, paradoxically, it is precisely the politics of positivism. The establishment to legitimize itself often uses its scientific nature. In other words, positivism can prove to be pro-establishment, status-quoist, non-critical and non-reflexive.

Post modernists

Post modernists deconstruct the very foundation of science. No wonder, for them, positivism loses its cognitive power and legitimacy. And in a way the distinction between objective science and subjective narrative gets eroded, sociological study becomes yet another narrative filled with biographies and life histories, and a non-positivist/post-modern sociological study does not look fundamentally different from cultural studies (discussed in detail in chapter ten).

Part III

Contemporary Social Theory

7

Functional Theory

There is a tradition in the field of social research that has variously been named as "functionalism," "structural functionalism," "the functional approach," "functional orientation," "functional analysis," and "functional theory." The antecedent of functional orientations in sociological inquiry was illustrated by a dictum of Voltaire, 'if there were no God, it would be necessary for man to invent one,' that is, belief in God is functionally indispensable to man. But, the real impetus to the employment of the term function came with those nineteenth-century social theorists like Auguste Comte and Herbert Spencer who regarded groups of societies or individual societies as being very similar to biological organisms in the way in which they worked. Emile Durkheim in turn argued that any sociological explanation should consist of the discovery, firstly, of a phenomenon's cause and, secondly, of its function. Durkheim said,

> "We use the word "function" in preference to "end" or "purpose," precisely because social phenomena do not generally exist for the useful results they produce. We must determine whether there is a correspondence between the fact under consideration and the general needs of the social organism, and in what this correspondence consists, without occupying ourselves with whether it has been intentional or not" (quoted in Robertson 1981: 86).

Hence, the basic premise of functional theory was not in the transformation of human society, and to treat 'culture' as unified but were rooted in relativism and interdependence. It was believed that cultures are multiple and each is unique. The questions that were asked were not about origin and progress but about the contribution and function of each trait to the functioning of the whole. The whole here was a living society and culture to be studied only in the present with no allusion to the past or future.

The fundamental postulate of functionalism was that all social structures, or at least the major ones, contribute to the integration and adaptation of the system in which they operate. The existence or persistence of a given structure or pattern is explained by means of its consequences or effects, which are presumably both necessary and beneficial to the society in question. For them, a given pattern fulfills some vital "system need" and that this fulfilment "explains" the existence of the pattern (Zeitlin 1987: 3).

In order to understand social reality, the functional theorists favoured 'static theory.' A static explanation is one where a social variable is explained only in terms of variables belonging to the same time period. This kind of theory is not based on a premise that the phenomenon in question is actually a historical but on the assumption that a sufficient understanding of it is possible by recourse to data that are situational. Usually, the functionalists have explained what function is being performed by a particular trait in a particular culture at a particular period of time.

The leading representatives of functionalism were Bronislaw Malinowski, A. R. Radcliffe-Brown, Talcott Parsons (1902-1979) and Robert K. Merton. The 1920s witnessed a reorientation among cultural and social anthropologists; and this sprang particularly from the work of Bronislaw Malinowski, who was instrumental in establishing an approach which emphasized the importance of analyzing primitive societies as socio-cultural wholes, accounting for institutions in terms of their relations to other institutions in the same society and their significance in satisfying and meeting the basic needs, notably the biological needs of individual members. However, Malinowski was less important than A. R. Radcliffe-Brown with respect to the elaboration of the theoretical ramifications of a thoroughly social functionalism. Radcliffe-Brown frankly advocated the analogy between social life and organic life; although he tried to avoid Durkheim's emphasis on the 'needs' of the social organism and spoke instead of 'necessary conditions of existence'. This was because he wished to avoid teleological implications, such as the notion of some 'guiding spirit' or mysterious force in social life. Radcliffe-Brown's work involved a distinction between social morphology, the analysis of the network of social relationships constituting social structure, and social physiology, the study of the working and persistence of all interrelated social phenomena in a society (Robertson 1981: 86).

Talcott Parsons (1902-1979): Action Theory and the Social System

The functionalist tradition attained its most systematic and rigorous formulation in Parsons's 'structural-functional' theory. In article published in 1935, entitled "The Place of Ultimate Values in Sociological Theory," Parsons laid out the main elements that he later elaborated in his first major work, *The Structure of Social Action* (1937) which is considered as one of the most influential theoretical works of the twentieth century. He provided a grand theory of social action and social order rooted in a society's "common value system" (Zeitlin 1987: 18) that dominated sociological thinking in the mid-twentieth century. In one of his earliest outlines of this theory, written in 1944, he argued that the significance of the concept of function inhered in its potential for the linking of the structural categories of sociology. Without such a concept the analyst was prone to give a static impression of social systems. A functional approach would produce criteria of the importance of factors and processes and their interrelationships within the system as a 'going concern' (Robertson 1981: 86).

Parsons held that theory in sociological research must be built up around a limited number of important concepts that are adequate to grasp the objective and external social reality. These concepts are analytical constructs abstracted from empirical reality. Thus Parsons tried to develop a naturalistic/positivistic conceptual schema. Underlying Parsons' method of building theoretical analysis was the assumption that the social reality does have systematic regularities that can be analytically grasped. At the same time he advocated the existence of the complex symbolic functioning of the human mind. He considered personality as an aspect of the socio-cultural system and there is a "common sector" of both the personality and the social system. According to him, "it consists in the value-patterns which define role expectations. The motivational structures thus organized are units *both* of personality as a system and of the social system in which the actor participates; they are need-dispositions of the personality and they are role-expectations of the social system. This is key to the "transformational formula" between the two systems of personality and social system.

Parsons argued, "The fundamental relationships between need-dispositions of the personality, role-expectations of the social system and internalized-institutionalized value-patterns of the culture, is the fundamental nodal point of the organization of systems of action" (1951: 540). The entire interaction process is mediated by a "system of culturally structured and shared symbols" (1951: 6). For him, the "three basic modes of motivational orientation" or major aspects of action were what he calls the *cognitive, cathectic, and evaluative.* For Parsons, the *cognitive* refers to the actor's definition of the situation in terms of his interests; the *cathectic*, the actor's quest for gratification; and the *evaluative,* to the actor's choice and ordering of alternatives. An actor may wait for events to take place, a state called "anticipation"; or he may seek actively to bring them about or avoid them, a state called "goal-directedness" which he considers as being "a fundamental property of all action-systems"(1951: 8). Thus, at the core of his voluntaristic theory of action is the thinking and individual actor, who is goal seeking. This goal seeking behaviour is faced with alternative means and situated in varying life conditions that act as constraints on the goal seeking behaviour. The actors are also governed by values, norms and ideas that influence choice of goals as well as the appropriate means to achieve them. Finally action involves actors making subjective decisions to choose the means to achieve the goals under the given conditions of constraint (1951: 9).

Parsons' action theory rests on the fundamental postulate that human social interaction is based on complex and abstract system of symbolic communication, notably language but also the other shared symbolic meanings of the cultural tradition. A most important element of this shared tradition may be called a "value," "which serves as a criterion or standard for selection among the alternatives of orientation which are intrinsically open in a situation" (1951: 12). According to him, three logically independent systems, the social, the cultural, and the personal, are therefore involved in action. In other words, Parsons' action theory is integrative in nature and his concepts of functional prerequisites are independent of time or place. They are general and a historical, that is, they are found in all societies at any point of time.

In *Sociological Theory and Modern Society,* Parsons stated that "an evolutionary universal is a complex of structures and associated processes the development of which so increases the long-run adaptive capacity of living organisms in a given class that only systems that develop the complex can attain certain higher levels of general adaptive capacity" (1967: 493). Unlike the "natural selection," the relatively disadvantage do survive. For him, the criterion in the sociological realm is not necessarily the extinction of the unadaptive societies (Zeitlin 1987: 52). He continues, "these four features of even the simplest action system – religion, communication with language, social organization through kinship, and technology – may regarded as an integrated set of evolutionary universals at even the earliest human level. No known human society has existed without *all* four in relatively definite relations to each other. In fact their presence constitutes the very minimum that may be said to mark a society as truly human" (Parsons 1967: 495).

A critique has commented that Parsons' views on functionalism were not without its problem. "For as he proceeds to elaborate the system side of his action theory, Parsons employs all the functionalist assumptions and terms that we found to be so problematic from several standpoints. Parsons recognizes that a scientific theory of social system requires criteria for their empirical separation; his success in providing them, however, is no greater than of the other functionalists" (Zeitlin 1987: 23). In *Societies: Evolutionary and Comparative Perspectives,* Parsons asserted that he is not "merely reviving old ideas" and that he has considered "the idea of social evolution in the context of the major theoretical and empirical advances that have accumulated since the earlier evolutionists wrote" (Parsons 1966: 109). However, he does not specify what these advances have been, though he believes that his own formulation has successfully avoided what he calls the deadly sin of the nineteenth-century thinkers, namely, monism, or theories based on single factor (Zeitlin 1987: 50). Anthony Giddens has pointed out that "in both Althusserian Marxism and Parsonian sociology the reproduction of society occurs 'behind the backs' of the agents whose conduct constitutes that society. The involvement of actors' own purposive conduct with the rationalization of action is lacking in each case: in Parson's sociology as a result of the value-consensus-norm-internalized-need-disposition theorem, and in Althusser's writings as a consequence of his deterministic account of agency; hence the teleology of the system either governs (in the first) or supplants (in the second) that of actors themselves" (1979: 112).

Robert K. Merton (1910-2003): Revision of Functionalism

The most important criticism of functionalism came out from within the limits of functionality. In *Social Theory and Social Structure,* published in 1968, Merton criticised the traditional functionalist postulates and concepts. These include: firstly, that standardized social activities or cultural items are functional for the *entire* social or cultural system; secondly, that *all* such social or cultural items fulfil sociological functions; and thirdly, that these items are consequently indispensable (1968: 79). He postulated that a society's unity ought not to be posited in advance but ought rather to be an empirical question. One must specify the unit for which a given item is functional; and one must beware of accepting as an unqualified postulate the view that all items fulfil vital functions. He argued that functional analysis must allow for diverse consequences, including dysfunctions as well as functions. *Functions*, he viewed, are those observed consequences which make for the adaptation or adjustment of a given system; *dysfunctions*, those observed consequences which lesson the adaptation or adjustment of the system (1968: 105).

Function has two dominant meanings in social research. Its major use is to be seen in the following statement: 'The social function of religion is the maintenance of group solidarity.' Here function refers to the diagnosed objective consequence which a social phenomenon has for a wider system of which it is a part. Manifest functions are objective consequences for the system which are intended and recognized by the relevant participants; and, latent functions are neither intended nor recognized. In order to distinguish between activities which contribute, on the one hand, to survival of social system patterns and, on the other, to their disturbance, a distinction is made respectively between eufunctions and dysfunctions. There are thus manifest and latent eufunctions and manifest and latent dysfunctions (Robertson 1981: 85).

Finally, one must not assume that one and only one item or structure can fulfill a given function. Rather, social scientists should allow for the fact "that alternative social structures (and cultural forms) have served ... the function necessary for the persistence of groups. Proceeding further, we must set forth a major theorem of functional analysis; *just as the same item may have multiple functions, so may the same functions be diversely fulfilled by alternatives items"* (1968: 87-88, italics in original). He argued that "we have observed the difficulties entailed in *confining* analysis to functions fulfilled for 'the society,' since items may be functional for some individuals and subgroups and dysfunctional for others. It is necessary, therefore, to consider a *range* of units for which the item has designated consequences: individuals in diverse statutes, subgroups, the larger social system and cultural systems" (1968: 106). But Merton has been criticized for retaining in his "paradigm for functional analysis" the very concepts he himself describes as "the cloudiest and most debatable," namely, "prerequisites," "system-needs," "adaption," and the like. In fact, Merton's revisions have not answered the major objections to traditional functionalists. A critique has pointed out, "are civil rights demonstration functions or dysfunctions?" (Sorokin 1966: 450).

Since Merton's "Manifest and Latest Functions' (1949), there have been two major variants of sociological functionalism. Merton helped to precipitate the establishment of a perspective which was less committed to the stability, consensus, and integration foci of structural-functionalism (Robertson 1981: 87). Thus whilst most sociologists are social functionalists in respect of their concern with systems comprising interdependent parts, and their interest in the unintended social consequences of social action and organization, and also their refusal to reduce the analysis of social life to the psychological level, only structural-functionalists base their work on the highly abstract conception of the normatively integrated system (Ibid.: 88).

However, the entire concept of functionality and harmony were questioned on methodological grounds of teleology, and on ethical grounds of social injustice, that is to say, does functionality guarantee justice? Teleology refers to justifying the existence of a phenomenon by the function it performs. It implies that one is trying to explain the effect as the cause of a phenomenon. This is precisely what functionalists did by way of offering explanations of social phenomena. But, functionality does not guarantee justice. For example, even slavery may have been a functional system in that it was productive and it worked, but to call it just would be stretching things too far.

8

Structuralism

In structuralist doctrine the crucial feature which distinguishes human beings, "man in culture," from animals of the species Homo, "man in nature," is the possession of language which is both natural, in that our ability to speak is a genetic endowment, and cultural, in that any particular language serves to distinguish members of one culture from members of another. Language, as uttered in words either verbally or in writing, is a projection into the external world of conceptual patterns in the mind of the speaker. And by analogy this is true also of all other cultural manifestations; our tools, our clothes, our houses, the way we arrange our settlements, the way we prepare our food, our 'manners and customs' in all their aspects, are all human products generated by human minds. Consequently the interrelations which are discernible objectively in such manifest features of culture must correspond in some way to relational characteristics of the minds which produced them in the first place.

The structuralists applied a similar kind of analysis to non-verbal features of customary behaviour. They argued that all such customary behaviours, which the participant actors take entirely for granted, in fact reflect patterned permutations among a range of limited possibilities and that such patterned operations, if considered collectively as sets rather than one at a time, will be seen to be structured in positive and negative instances, rather like a morse code, and that the pattern as a whole will tell us significant facts about the workings of the human mind (Peters 1981: 222-23).

Claude Levi-Strauss (1908-2009)

Levi-Strauss, a French anthropologist, is normally considered to be the founding figure of structuralism in social sciences and human sciences. He applied the methods of structural linguistics to social phenomena. He was profoundly influenced by the Swiss linguistics Ferdinand de Saussure who is generally recognized as the father of modern linguistics; and the phonological method developed by the Russian linguists Trubetzkoy and Jakobson. He drew from them the rules of procedure: concentrate not on conscious phenomena but on their unconscious infrastructure; do not attribute an independent value to the elements of a system but rather a positional meaning, that is to say, the value of the elements is dependent upon the relations that combine and oppose them, and these relations must be the foundations of the analysis (Pouillon 2004: 571). An important feature of Levi-Strauss's definition of structure is that, like Saussure's *langue*, it is independent of the conscious intentions and interpretations of the individual member of the social group. He asserted that it is unconscious in the same way that implicit rules of a language are not conscious to the average speaker of the language.

In his first major work, *The Elementary Structures of Kinship,* published in 1949 he emphasized that the way the phonologist has reduced the diversity of sounds in natural languages to a limited set of basic distinctions, so the anthropologist/social scientist should be able to reduce the many different permutations of kinship relations observed in human society to a small group of elementary and invariant structures from which the diversity of observable kinship structures might be derived.

For example, among speakers of the English language, utterance of the word son carries significance for both speaker and listener because of a patterned structure of relationships with a number of other words belonging to the same set such as: father, mother, husband, wife, daughter, brother, sister. The word son does not mean anything by itself; we credit it with meaning because, unconsciously, we are able to contrast it with other terms and then, again subconsciously, compare and contrast such relationships as mother-son, sister-brother; father-son, brother-brother; mother-son, mother-daughter; husband-wife, brother-sister, mother's brother (uncle), sister's son (nephew), and so on. The total cultural significance of the single word son is embedded in the structure of this total complex of contrasted relationships which Lévi-Strauss refers to as 'the atom of kinship.'

In 1950s Lévi-Strauss went on to extend this application of the linguistic model to the field of collective representations. He argued for the *symbolic* nature of social customs and institutions. The collective constructs that mediate relationships between the different members of a community are symbolic to the extent that their construction is a matter of arbitrary convention and that they form discrete systems with their own 'grammar' or rules of operation. Collective representations such as totemism or myth could therefore be analysed in same way as language. In *Totemism* (1962) and *The Savage Mind* (1962) he argued that whereas traditional interpretations of totemism focussed on the mystical link between individual and totem, the structuralist interpretation looked at totemism as a kind of 'code' based on structural homology between natural species and social groups. Structurally, each myth was a more or less distant transforms of another myth, so that the totality of myths generated by the human mind could be said to represent a closed system. He asserted, it is not individuals that speak through myths but myths that speak through individuals.

Another closely related structuralist principle is that of transformation. Patterns of behaviour which are generated as manifest cultural products in the real objective world are generated by 'deep' unconscious structures in human minds or perhaps even by a universal collectivity 'the human mind', which is a shared natural characteristic of all human beings. If the reductionist argument is carried that far, then it must follow that the varieties of cultural product which are generated in the real world must all be transformations of each other since all of them derive from the same ultimate structured source in the human unconscious. At this level there are close parallels between the theories of the structuralists and those of the Freudian psycho-analysts but Lévi-Strauss has gone much further than Freud in that he claims to be able to decipher the transformation rules which will convert the modalities of one culture into the modalities of another (Ibid.).

Since mid-1950s, the structuralism of Levi-Strauss has been immensely influential in the social science research, and in a wide spectrum of humanities disciplines as evident in the psychoanalysis of Jacques Lacan, the 'structural history' of Fernand Braudel, the 'deconstruction' of Michel Foucault and the literary studies of Roland Barthes. Together, this constellation of thinkers was seen in the 1960s and 1970s to constitute structuralist movement, with Levi-Strauss as their leading figure (Johnson 2004: 1010-12).

9

Critical Theory

The term "social conflict" at its most general level, embraces an array of phenomena from interpersonal disagreement and quarrels through class conflict and including, as well, international rivalry and war (Zeilin 1987: 104). There is no unanimity on the term "conflict theory" and it is not difficult to see it covers several heterogeneous and even contradictory perspectives (Martindale 1960: 127).

Lewis A. Coser (1913-2003): Functionalized Conflict

Coser recognizes that there is no extant theory of social conflict that includes all these phenomena. Nor does he wish to construct such a general theory. Instead, he regards his work, *The Functions of Social Conflict*, published in 1956, "an effort to clarify the concept of social conflict" and "to consolidate conceptual schemes which are pertinent to data of social conflict." He defined social conflict as "a struggle over values and claims to status, power and resources in which the aims of the opponents are to neutralize, injure or eliminate their rivals." He writes "our concern is mainly with the with the functions, rather than the dysfunctions, of social conflict, that is to say, with those consequences of social conflict which make for an increase rather than a decrease on the adaptation or adjustment of particular social relationships or groups"(1956: 7-8). According to him, "social conflict has been severely neglected; insofar, as sociologists have treated it, the emphasis has been on its 'negative' side – how it undermines order, stability, and unity." Rather, he emphasized on the "positive" side of the conflict, that is, how it contributes to the maintenance and "adaptation" of social groups, relationships and systems, that is to say, conflict is "positively functional for the social structures." He suggested that "whereas conflict changes the terms of interaction, mere expression of hostile feelings does not. Thus, expression, as distinct from conflict, may be welcomed by the powers that be" (1956: 44). He opined that "an institution which serves to channel hostility and to prevent release against the original object, thereby maintaining the structure of the social system, may also have serious dysfunctions for either the social system or the actor or both" (1956: 45). Furthermore, "institution which offer substitute channel for the release of aggressiveness may be dysfunctional for the social system in the same way as neurotic symptoms are dysfunctional for the personality system" (1956: 46). Continuing, he writes, "Internal social conflicts which concern goals, values, or interests that do not contradict the basic assumptions upon which the relationships is founded tend to be positively functional for the social structures" (1956: 151).

Coser concluded that conflict is "dysfunctional for a social structure in which there is no or insufficient toleration or institutionalization of conflict. The intensity of a conflict which threatens to 'tear apart,' which attacks the consensual basis of a social system, is related to the rigidity of the structure. What threatens the equilibrium of such structure is not conflict as such, but the rigidity itself which permits hostilities to accumulate and be channelled along one major line of cleavage once they break out in conflict" (1956: 157). However, as pointed out by a critic, whenever these original ideas are translated into "functionalese," they gain nothing and lose their incisiveness" (Zeitlin 1987: 107).

Ralf G. Dahrendorf (1929-2009): Postcapitalist Society

Dahrendorf is among the best-known contemporary representatives of the "conflict theory." In *Class and Conflict in Industrial Society,* published in 1959, he postulated that his conflict theory is "applicable to the analysis of the political process both in totalitarian and in free societies of the present" by providing new definition of class conflict based on authority relations. He criticized Marx's two-class model of the capitalist system. For him, Marx's "analyses are essentially based on narrow, legal concept of property." He argued that "for Marx the real criterion of class was ownership and non-ownership of the means of production in the strict and legalistic sense, and not the authority structure of the enterprise" (Zeitlin 1987: 110). Only by freeing class from this "narrow" definition will it become "applicable to all relations of production" (1959: 21). Dahrendorf supported his case by drawing attention to Marx's treatment, in the third volume of *Capital*, of joint-stock company, which in Marx's time had already exhibited the tendency later described as the separation of ownership and control. Dahrendorf believed that "for Marx, the relations of production as a determinant of class formation were also authority relations, but they were such only because in the first place they were property relations in the narrow sense of the distribution of controlling private ownership" (1959: 22). He argued that structural changes since Marx's time have rendered his theoretical approach useless; and he tried to substitute a theory of conflict and change that will be "applicable not merely to capitalist societies but to industrial societies in general" (1959: 36).

For Dahrendorf, the dominance of the corporation and the dispersion of stock constitute a total break with capitalism. He calls the process of separation of ownership from control as the "decomposition of capital." In his opinion, "the enterprise owned and run by an individual, or even a family, has long ceased to be dominant pattern of economic organization. Moreover, the stock of companies is dispersed widely" (1959: 42). Like James Burnham, he regarded the emergence of corporation as a managerial revolution, or the beginning of the end of capitalism (Zeitlin 1987: 113). He acknowledges that property has not altogether "ceased to function as a basis of authority. The right to manage command and expect obedience accrues in part from the property rights delegated to him by shareholders, acting either as a group or through an elected board of directors." But there is a "second, and more important, basis of legitimacy for his authority, namely, some kind of consensus among those who are bound to obey his command" (1959: 45). To quote Dahrendorf: "capital and thereby capitalism has dissolved and given way, in the economic spheres, to a plurality of partly agreed, partly competing, and partly simply different groups" (1959: 47). There has occurred a decomposition of labour which implies a growing heterogeneity and even conflict of interests among industrial workers-so much so that, "as with the capitalist class, it has doubtful of the working class still makes much sense" (1959: 51).

Moreover, the emergence of "new middle class," that is to say, the phenomenal growth of the white-collar work force has provided the heterogeneous groupings what C. Wright calls an "occupational salad" may be divided into two quasi-classes: those who command and those who obey. In other words, the growth of the new groupings of bureaucrats and white-collar workers is another significant structural change that has occurred since Marx's time. Besides these, the other structural changes include: social mobility, equality, and the institutionalization of class conflict. Dahrendorf pointed out that "in post-capitalist societies there is great deal of movements , upwards and downwards as well as on social level, between generations as well as within them, so that the individual who stays at his place of birth and in the occupation of his father throughout his life has become rare exception" (1959: 59). Continuing, he writes, there is remarkable spread of social equality from the point of view of legal privileges and deprivations, as every citizens of advanced industrial societies has an equal status; and by the simultaneous rise of real wages of workers and the taxation of top earnings a redistribution of income has taken place (1959: 61-63).

Furthermore, Dahrendorf pointed out that the power, domination, and conflict have not ceased to exist in the post-capitalist societies as there are those who control strategic resources and, therefore, command, and others who obey. Wherever there is authority, there are relations of domination and subordination. But, he viewed the contemporary post-capitalist societies as plurality of relatively discreet "imperatively coordinated associations" in which "the state, a church, an enterprise, but also a political party, a trade union, and a chess club are associations in this sense" (1959: 168). In all such associations a definite dichotomy exists between some who have authority and others who have none. But, according to him, these conflicts are institutionalized, regulated, and insulated from the society at large; and "domination in one association does not necessarily involve domination in all others to which he belongs, and subjection, conversely, in one does not mean subjection in all" (1959: 171). However, Dahrendorf's thesis has been criticized on the ground that "in the European industrial countries, and to a lesser extent in the USA, the major political conflicts are closely and continuously associated with industrial conflicts, and express the divergent interests of the principal social classes" (Bottomore 1966: 27). Also, the state is not a mere association, and in the wide range of circumstances state authority supersedes all other associations.

10

Post Modernism

Post modernism is a term applied to a wide-ranging set of developments in critical theory, philosophy, architecture, art, literature, and culture, which are generally characterized as emerging from, in reaction to, or superseding, modernism. It has been used variably to refer to what are interpreted as major changes in the way the contemporary world can and ought to be represented. The term, introduced from architecture and art criticism, which then passed into philosophy and literary studies, has now become something of a commonplace in the social sciences. In architecture, where it first gained currency, postmodernism referred to an active break with the principle tenets of modern architecture and the emergence of now combinations of older styles, the return of concrete as opposed to abstract forms, the active use of kitsch and pastiche (Friedman 2004: 777).

The recognition of the process of "construction" was contingent upon the process of "deconstruction" which is a strategy of critical analysis closely associated with Jacques Derrida (1930-2004). It aims to expose unquestioned metaphysical assumptions and internal contradictions in philosophical and literary language. He especially avoided defining the term and resisted the attempts of later academics to turn "deconstruction" into a coherent strategy or system. The reason was that the deconstructive approach challenges the transparency of language, and especially the ability to ever arrive at a single final meaning of a word. So the proponents of deconstructive approach would object to such definition. Derrida introduced what is now commonly called a deconstructive reading, in which he attempted to describe many different "voices" in certain pivotal western philosophical and cultural contexts, without classifying them into binary oppositions or hierarchies, which he believed were hallmarks of western thought.

According to Jean-Francis Lyotard (1924-1998), post modernity is characterized as "incredulity toward meta-narratives." He announced the demise of the great paradigm of scientific rationality and the return of multiple wisdoms, cultures, and a relativism of knowledge. In *The Post Modern Condition: A Report on Knowledge* (1979), Lyotard opined that in the era of post modern culture, people have rejected the grand, supposedly universal stories and paradigms such as religion, conventional philosophy, capitalism and gender that have defined culture and behaviour in the past and have instead begun to organize cultural life around a variety of more local and sub-cultural, myths and stories. Furthermore, it promotes the idea that all such meta-narratives and paradigms are stable only while they fit the available evidence, and can potentially be overturned when phenomena occur that the paradigm cannot account for, and a better explanatory model (itself subject to same fate) is found. For Lyotard, it was liberation from the straitjacket of rationalist purity of the master discourses of a totalitarian modernity. In his *Philosophy and the Mirror of Nature* (1980), Richard Rorty, another early representative of philosophical postmodernism, stressed the impossibility of scientific models of progress and argued for 'edifying conversation' among paradigms rather than cumulative development.

The early discussions in the social sciences was very much intertwined with the more general philosophical discussions and was especially focused on Habermas's critique of Lyotard, Bell and others, and the ensuing debate between proponents of postmodernism versus modernism. In *The Philosophical Discourse of Modernity* (1987), Habermas stated that postmodernism was a dangerously conservative rejection of the incomplete modern project, a capitulation to the apparent failure of the emancipatory content of the project. During the 1980s, much of the discussions concerned the pros and cons of post modernism as an intellectual position. Subsequently the discussion moved towards an attempt at interpreting the social conditions themselves. There are numerous interpretations of the 'post modern condition'. For some it is an aspect of what Bell referred to as post-industrialization, the movement from mass industrial towards information-based technology and the emergence of an information society in which control of communication was to become central. In *The Cultural Contradictions of Capitalism* (1976), Bell mentioned that the postmodern is a product of modernism itself, the effect of the destruction of meaning, of morality, of authoritative structures, leading ultimately to 'pornotopia'. In his book, *In the Shadow of the Silent Majorities* (1983), Baudrillard argued that with the advent of information technology symbolic meaning is disappearing, being replaced by a plethora of floating signifies where the social is reduced to simulacra. His interpretation represents a world devoid of meaning in which there is little hope in the future, whereas for other approaches (e.g. Lyotard) the postmodern is the advent of a non-hegemonic political and intellectual strategy.

The proponents of postmodernism have openly attacked modernism as a hegemonic discourse, a structure of control and domination in which discipline was instated by way of rationality itself. (Friedman 2004: 778). Attempts to come to grips with the social transformations underlying the apparent decline of modernity are represented by Lash and Urry (1987) and Harvey (1990). In *The End of Organized Capitalism* (1987) Lash and Urry argued that the decline of modernity is part of a general process of disorganization of capitalism, a fragmentation of formerly hierarchical processes leading to various forms of social disorder, and a demand for flexibility. In *The Condition of Postmodernity* (1990) Harvey stated that the major process involved in the time-space compression produced by an increasingly rapid process of capitalist reproduction on a global scale. Vattimo (1987), in another important analysis of the degeneration of modernity, has tried to link postmodernism to the decline of Western hegemony and the emergence of multiple political voices in the centre itself (Friedman 2004: 778).

As evident, in the post-nineteen-seventies era, the notions of deconstruction and de-structuralization spread across all fields of humanities, literature and art. The fixed faith in the definition of knowledge as that generated by western science was challenged, so was the so-called "progress" embodied in western civilization. The entire notion that knowledge exists as "facts" that can be established with the help of western scientific methods, and even that there is a fixed "reality" out there, was criticized. As a result, a major change took place in theory across the world and across social science theory with a total changeover in perspective occurred in the form of postmodernism that subjected the textual matter to a reflexive critique that goes into the politics of the construction of a text. All that has been written down is now viewed, not as descriptions of the "truth" per se but as constructions based upon the history, politics and strategy of authorship. Every concept taken for granted in the modernist era is now subjected to scrutiny. Culture, for example, is no longer to be viewed as a fixed entity, the symbolic representation of the mind of an identifiable group of people, but a shifting and contested process by which new identities are constructed.

In the field of social research, post modernism is described as being the result of economic, cultural and demographic changes. Related terms in this context include post industrial society, late capitalism, and it is attributed to factors: the rise of service economy, the importance of mass media and the rise of an interdependent world economy. As a cultural movement, post modernism is an aspect of post modernity, which is broadly defined as the condition of western society after modernity. The reason for this radical departure from modernism was the failure of western science and systems of knowledge to deliver the goods in a world threatened with environmental disasters, failure of civil society and deepening inequalities and injustice across the world. Another reason was the emergence of scholars from various race, class, ethnic, and gender categories. The central figure of the white and male scholar was displaced and taken over by a variety of others, who challenged the truth status of the findings. In the forefront were what is known as the colonial critique and the feminist critique. A new generation of scholars confronted the political and economic realities of 'colonial knowledge' by following the motivations and power equations involved in the knowledge. For an example, a radical departure in theoretical approach was a rewriting of history, of which the best examples in India are the series of books in *The New Cambridge History of India* and the series of books on subaltern history under the editorial leadership of Ranajit Guha (1982). Examples of what is known as the colonial critique and also a subaltern approach to history is reflected in the works of Partha Chattterjee (1993), Bernard Cohn (1996), Nicholas Dirks (1992) and others of the genre. The writings of Edward Said (1977) inspired many of the abovementioned works.

The strongly critical point of view of feminism is reflected in Stanley and Wise's (1983) definition of feminism as directly confronting the idea that one person or set of people have the right to impose definitions of reality on others. This also makes it compatible with the post modern concept of reality as situational. Another stand taken by post modernism was to resituate the researcher vis-à-vis the researched more equally. The researched was no longer reduced to the status of a passive "object of research" but became an equal partner in the production of knowledge. The sisterhood proclaimed by feminists was also related to an understanding of equality that could be achieved only if the producers of knowledge were from hitherto 'silenced' groups. The prominent feminist writer of colour, Audre Lorde (1934-1992) is of the opinion that any discussion of feminist theory that ignores the perspectives of women of colour, poor women and lesbians is suffering from academic arrogance (see Lorde 1989). Postmodernists, especially feminists, questioned the status of knowledge as value neutral, vertically arranged, privileging the researcher and divorced from action. The activist scholar became an integral part the late twentieth century academic world. Theory was finally liberated from its ivory tower and came down to the streets.

Thus, it could be argued that what is often designated as postmodernism is an aspect of the fragmentation of the global system. Here there is a link between the decentralization of capital accumulation, the decline of western hegemony, the decline of modernism as a strategic identity of self-development, and the emergence of multivocality, multiculturalism and of indigenous, Fourth World movements. There is an interesting parallel among different sets of fragmentations: the fragmentation of knowledge into separate relative fields, the disintegration of the evolutionary scheme of social types into a plethora of different cultures that have been interpreted as incommensurable with respect to one another, the real 'ethnification' of the nation-state, both as a result of regionalization and immigration, the apparent rise of so-called narcissistic disorders that might be indicative of the dissolution of individual ego structures. The individual is also subject to changes in conditions of existence that in their turn after practices of identification and meaning construal. This is the key to understanding the relation between economic and social processes, and cultural phenomena characteristic of postmodernity (Friedman 2004: 779).

11

Phenomenology

The term phenomenology is derived from the conjunction of the noun form of *phainomai,* to appear, and *logos* or reason. It treats consciousness as a given datum upon which we may build the foundations of claims to knowledge. Here is a presumption of an unmediated access to consciousness. The focus is on explaining the nature of practical consciousness. The intention is to reject *a priori* constructions and pay attention to the description of experience. This involves a description of the physical actions of the actors as well as their intentions and purposes, the way they make classification, attribute senses and meanings to their world.

The origins of human reason are to be discovered in the structure of appearance, and in the basic ordering of human experience. This emphasis serves to differentiate phenomenology from two other major streams of thought in modern philosophy: analytic philosophy and structuralism. Analytic philosophy gives pride of place to the logical form of language as the channel through which philosophical problems should be approached; structuralists place a stress upon the significance of unconscious principles of the organization of knowledge that are prior to conscious experiences. In contrast to each of these, for phenomenology the act of understanding has primacy of place; the capacity of the human mind to understand meaning is more basic than either formal logic or the modes in which knowledge is articulated or structured (Mitchell 1981: 141).

In the late nineteenth century, a group of Austrian philosophers grew dissatisfied with the excessive subjectivity fostered by the philosophy of the later German idealists. The Austrian philosophers were against excessive analysis of experiences. Instead of looking for causes and theories they concentrated on experiences as they present themselves to consciousness, without recourse to theory, deduction, or assumptions from other disciplines such as the natural sciences. Franz Brentano (1838-1917) was the first scholar to develop the basic approach of phenomenology. Brentano claimed that the central concern of philosophy is to understand the nature and content of awareness in ways that illuminate the distinction between the mental and the non-mental. In his *Psychology from an Empirical Standpoint*, published in 1874, Brentano proposed that every mental act be understood to have a doubly significant representational function. The function is to both designate itself reflectively and a phenomenal objects intentionally. Indeed, this distinction between acts and their objects is the crucial distinction for Brentano, since "intentionality is the mark of the mental." One and the same phenomenal object can be intended by mental acts of different modalities, like believing, imagining, etc. Brentano held that although each intentional act is itself subjective, its intention is an objective thing or fact in the world.

Edmund Husserl (1859-1938): Transcendental Phenomenology

A disciple of Brentano, a German philosopher Edmund Husserl carried forward Brentano's ideas. Husserl introduced the term phenomenology in his book, *Ideas: A General Introduction to Pure Phenomenology* (1913; translated in 1931) and held that the task of phenomenology was to study essences, such as the essence of emotions. His transcendental phenomenology emphasized the essential foundations of knowledge in experience: an endeavour to formulate a basis for knowledge 'free from presuppositions'. He stated that only the essences of conscious structures are the proper subject matter of phenomenology. He defined phenomenology as the study of the structures of consciousness that enables consciousness to refer to object outside it. Such a study requires reflection on the content of the mind to the exclusion of everything else. He called this type of reflection the phenomenological reduction. Because the mind can be directed toward non-existent as well as real objects, He pointed out that phenomenological reflection does not presuppose that anything exists, but rather amounts to a "bracketing of existence", that is, setting aside the question of the real existence of the contemplated object.

What Husserl gathered when he contemplated the content of his mind were such acts as remembering, desiring, and perceiving and the abstract content of these acts, which Husserl called meanings. These meanings, he claimed, enabled an act to be directed toward an object under a certain aspect; and such directedness, called intentionality he held to be the essence of consciousness. For him, therefore, transcendental phenomenology was the study of the basic components of the meanings that make intentionality possible.

In order to unearth the essential elements of experience, Husserl held, we have to 'bracket', or 'think away' the everyday world (*Lebenswelt*) of the 'natural attitude', and concentrate upon the inner consciousness of the individual ego. Although he never abandoned this viewpoint, in his later work (especially in his *Crisis of the European Sciences and Transcendental Phenomenology,* part of which was published posthumously) he came to place more stress upon the direct study of the *Lebenswelt.* This helped initiate a second period in the development of phenomenology, so-called existential phenomenology or existentialism. The two leading influences here were the early writings of Heidegger (especially *Being and Time*, 1927) and Sartre (*Being and Nothingness*, 1943).

For Husserl the most important task is to develop a rigorous method that would enable the philosopher as scientist to get at the "things themselves." From the time of Locke, the empiricists, with their naturalistic attitude, mistakenly believed that they grasped reality, or things, directly, naively, and "immediately." Their inductive method, they thought, allowed for a direct contact with reality, unmediated by concepts. Knowledge was simply the cumulative recording of sensory impressions of reality, as it is, on a "mind" blank at birth. Mind, according to this view, was a relatively passive receptacle, a categoryless entity, playing no significantly active, organizing role in the development of knowledge. Husserl rejects this – as did Kant long before him– as naïve. The empiricists failed to recognize that their knowledge was mediated by concepts.

Husserl is, however, equally opposed to the Kantian view. Kant's contribution was revolutionary because he recognized the creative and constitutive qualities of mind and hence the subjective dimension of all knowledge. Like Kant, Husserl seeks the criterion of knowledge in the act of cognition. But more than this he cannot accept, rejecting resolutely Kant's *a priori* categories that forever hid the "things in themselves" from the knowing subject; and rejecting as well the Kantian dualism of the phenomenal and noumenal.

The really important task, as Husserl sees it, is to transcend both traditions by means of a radically new method that would facilitate an original intuition of the things themselves and a return to the immediate and original data of consciousness. Neither induction nor deduction but solely intuition of the primordial phenomena will yield valid knowledge undistorted by the presuppositions of the other sciences (Husserl 1965: 98). In these terms Husserl's philosophical ideal is a philosophy without presuppositions, an ideal that can be approached by the method he calls "reduction."

Hussserl argued, positive scientists, whether they are aware of it or not, provide us with an abstract and artificial structure of the world but not the world of our original experience. To break out of the artificial world of the positive sciences and to get at the world of our immediately experienced life (what Husserl calls the *Lebenswelt*), one needs to employ the method of "reduction" and to grasp a fundamental property of consciousness, namely, *intentionality* (a concept he took over from his teacher, Franz Brentano, but markedly transformed). Consciousness always directs itself towards that which it is not. It is the essence of consciousness to form meanings and to constitute its own objects.

Following Descartes, but again introducing modifications, Husserl wants to begin his philosophizing with radical doubt. One begins by calling into question everything previously taken for granted. This requires a different attitude (*Einstellung*) toward the world, looking at it with "new eyes." In his *Cartesian Meditations,* Husserl refers to this attitude as one in which one denies validity to the "natural belief in the existence of what" one experiences (1950: 59). One "invalidates," "inhibits," "disqualifies," all previously taken positions regarding the experienced objects. Finally, to quote Husserl's best-known phrase, one "brackets the objective world." Drawing his metaphor from mathematics, where one places an expression in brackets with a plus or minus sign before it, Husserl suggests that by bracketing the objective world one "gives it different value" (1913: 174). The "reduction" enables the phenomenologist to transform himself into a disinterested or disengaged observer.

"Reduction" also leads to the discovery of what Husserl calls the "transcendental ego." This is the "I" that ultimately decides sense and validity. In the process of intending objects other than itself it becomes aware of itself; it changes the world into mere phenomenon. The "I" becomes conscious of itself changing the world, but does not itself change. The "I" is pure ego, totally devoid of content and consisting of different forms of relatedness. In carrying out the "reduction" one does not reject or turn away from experienced reality; one simply suspends judgment about the reality and validity of the experience (Husserl 1950: 60). When one begins to reflect on this "reduced" world, one soon discovers that it is not one's private world but a world of meaning and value that has been intersubjectively constituted and to which one has consciously contributed (Edie 1967: 237). This intersubjectivity exists purely in the reflecting ego and is "constituted purely from the sources of my intentionality, but in such a manner that it is the *same* transcendental intersubjectivity in every single human being" (Schutz 1967: 126).

Martin Heidegger (1889-1976): Existential Phenomenology

Martin Heidegger, a German philosopher, employed the methods of phenomenology in pursuit of more comprehensive metaphysical goals. In Heidegger's full-fledged existentialism, the primary task of philosophy is to understand being itself, not merely our knowledge of it. Many feel that Heidegger's philosophy was more of statement on the existence of modern alienated humankind rather than any philosophical propositions. He felt that traditional learning focuses on 'what is', whereas it may be far more illuminating to examine the boundaries of ordinary knowledge by trying to study 'what is not.'

Heidegger (1963) held that it was only through the experience of nothingness that you are truly aware of something. For him traditional logic is no help, since it considers all negation as emanating from something positive. Heidegger proposed that we must abandon logic in order to explore the character of nothing as the background out of which everything emerges. Carefully contemplating nothing in itself, we begin to notice the importance and vitality of our own moods. Above all else, nothing is what produces in us a feeling of dread. This deep feeling of dread, Heidegger held, is the most fundamental human clue to the nature and reality of nothing. Heidegger was making a statement on ontology or existence rather than actually theorising on knowledge. Existential phenomenology rejects the search for transcendental categories of knowledge, and instead places the emphasis upon the nature of being within the *Lebenswelt*. Existentialism became a modish philosophy in post-War France, and was perceived as much more of a direct challenge to existing forms of social science, particularly by Marxists, than the earlier version of phenomenology had been.

Alfred Schutz (1899-1959): Phenomenology of the Social World

The phenomenological movement in philosophy had a great influence on sociological study. Such sociologists as Alfred Schutz have adapted it to promote an understanding of the relationship between states of individual consciousness and social life. As an approach within sociological study, phenomenology seeks to reveal how human awareness is implicated in the production of social action, social situations and social worlds. Alfred Schutz distilled from Husserl's rather dense writings a sociologically relevant approach. He set about describing how subjective meanings give rise to an apparently objective social world, in which the activities of everyday life have a duration or temporality. It comprises a continuity that remains throughout the waking hours of the individual's life. According to Schutz, individuals organise intentionality of their activities in terms of their overall priorities.

Schutz's major work, *The Phenomenology of the Social World*, was originally published in Austria in 1932, but with the outbreak of the War he emigrated to the United States, and it is there that his ideas have had their greatest impact. Schutz's works do not reflect the concern with problems of anxiety and moral commitment characteristic of Continental existentialism, but in some respects they otherwise share similar perspectives. According to Schutz, orthodox sociology has failed to recognize the significance of the everyday world of common-sense beliefs and practices as the basis of social reality. In studying the ways in which social actors 'typify' actions, and employ 'stocks of knowledge' to create 'a meaningful social world, we can open a new dimension to sociology. Schutz's version of phenomenology has been taken up and extended by Berger and Luckmann in a series of publications, most notably, *The Social Construction of Reality* (1966). Schutz's work is also one of the main sources of ethnomethodology, as elaborated by Garfinkel and others (Mitchell 1981: 142).

Schutz pointed out the essentials of the common-sense, taken-for-granted, everyday world - an elaboration of Husserl's *Lebénswelt*. He employed as well Husserl's notion of appresentation to explain how we come to know others and communicate with them. He commented, 'only the other's body is presented to me, not his mind. His conscious life is appresented, not presented. My consciousness receives indications of his conscious life and experiences mainly by visual perception of his body, his actions, and the actions of others upon him.' These well-ordered indications Husserl called a system of appresentations, which, in turn, he regarded as the source of sign systems and, ultimately, of language. In short, we grasp the physical body of the other as expressing his "spiritual I" - a concept roughly equivalent to Scheler's "person" and the symbolic interactionists' "self." He added, "It is towards this "I" and its motivational meaning that each of us directs his actions. When we say, for example, that we are in empathy with an other, it is the same as saying we have grasped his meaning through appresentation." He said,

> "This process is not unlike the one in which we find meaning in any cultural object, whether, this be a book, a tool, a house, or what-have-you. When I read a book it is clearly not to the book as material object that I orient myself, but to its meaning. It is the spiritual meaning of the object that we appresentationally apperceive and not its actual appearance. We constitute the object in accordance with the meaning it has for us. Similarly, in face-to-face interaction it is not the words merely as external sounds that we hear as we listen to someone talking but rather words as vehicles of meaning that enable us to comprehend him" (1967: 314).

When Schutz speaks of the microworld of "face-to-face" interaction, he also uses terms like "world within my actual reach" and "world within my manipulatory zone." The concepts, if not the actual words, are also employed by William James and George Herbert Mead. This microworld, the sector that comes within my actual reach and becomes my Here, is not the same as that which comes within your reach; that is, "your Here is my There." He elaborated, "True, our worlds may overlap, so that some things and events may be within the manipulatory zone of both of us. Yet the objects and events will appear differently from our respective standpoints as to their "direction, distance, perspective, adumbration, etc...." (1967: 315). The common sense, taken-for-granted attitude we share is that we could exchange places and that if we did so each would then see the world just as the other did previously. Of course, this applies, he argued, not only to spatial but also to socio-cultural perspectives.

Schutz explained, each enters the relationship with only a fragment of his personality, that is, by assuming a specific role. Their respective systems of relevance, resulting from their biographically unique situations, can never be totally congruent; Ego can never make Alter's system of relevance really his own, he can merely understand it. For all these reasons you and I transcend each other's worlds. There is, however, still another form of transcendence that becomes evident with the "We-relation." This phenomenon, says Schutz, belongs to the realm of meaning transcending everyday life and can only be grasped symbolically (1967: 317).

Schutz regarded 'the practical everyday "world of working" as the paramount reality, for this is the area of social life in which men treat the world as a field to be dominated, and strive to overcome the resistance of objects and others to their life plans.' This is the reality we are all most interested in, but not all aspects of this paramount world are equally relevant to our life projects. We select from the world within our actual or potential reach those objects that we believe will serve our interests and the realization of our projects (1967: 226).

Moreover, he put forward that men orient themselves and cope with the everyday world by means of commonsense constructs and thought objects. Inevitably, then, the social scientist's constructs refer not to a mindless, meaningless world, but to a socially constructed world of meaning. This means, he wrote, "the constructs used by the social scientist are, so to speak, constructs of the second degree, namely constructs of the constructs made by the actors on the social scene, whose behaviour the scientist observes and tries to explain in accordance with the procedural rules of his science" (1967: 6).

For Schutz, the natural and social worlds are therefore structured differently. From this, however, he does not conclude that a social science is impossible or that it is based on fundamentally different rules of procedure. He dissociates himself both from those who deny the possibility of a social science and from those who have opted for a behaviourist method that ignores or radically departs from the common-sense concepts men employ in their everyday lives. For Schutz, the social sciences present special difficulties that may be overcome through specific methodological devices. In this respect he follows Weber, but supplements Weber's typology of action with phenomenological insights (Zeitlin 1987: 176).

According to Schutz, 'All sciences, the physical as well as the social, employ abstractions and study typical, and not unique events.' The social sciences are justified in doing so 'since Everyman in everyday life also employs abstractions and orients himself in terms of typical facts, events, and experiences.' What is it, then, that makes the 'social sciences different and what is it that imposes special obligations upon them? For him, the special problem and responsibility of the social sciences is "to develop methodological devices for attaining objective and verifiable knowledge of a subjective meaning structure" (1967: 36). This requires a special posture on the social scientist's part as well as systematic attention to the relation of the typical constructs of common sense to those of social science. Because the observer's interest in this situation is different from that of the actors themselves, and because his purpose in seeking understanding is also different, his constructs also differ from theirs.

Schutz summarized, the social scientist, therefore, is a special case of disinterested observation. He, too, presumably, has no vital or practical interest in the situation he observes, only a cognitive or theoretical one. He is uninvolved in the hopes and fears of the participants and shares none of their anxiety about the outcome of their actions. He is, in short, "detached." To be sure, the social scientist always remains a participant in the social world and is therefore always interested, involved or engaged in some aspect of it. In a society consisting of classes, strata, groups, and associations, there can be no doubt that he will inevitably favour the values and interests of some and oppose those of others. Schutz would therefore agree that the social scientist is never absolutely detached. So, in terms quite similar to Husserl's "reduction," Scheler's and Mannheim's "disinterestedness" and "relatively unattached intellectuals," and Weber's "value-neutrality", Schutz also emphasizes that disinterestedness is a matter of *attitude*. It is an ideal posture towards which the social scientist should strive (Zeitlin 1987: 179).

12

Hermeneutics

Having reached the stage of the rules of interpretation, to interpret well we have to linguistically contextualize the utterances of the writer, as well as historically contextualize the writer. We are still puzzled. What do the rules of the interpretation of texts have to do amid social research? Don't they belong instead to such disciplines as literary criticism? To answer to these questions Thompson commented, "In the wake of their work, the text to be interpreted was no longer a mere fragment of classical or Christian literature, but rather history itself as the document of the achievements and failures of humanity" (1981: 37). Rather, Thompson's words echo the great German historians, Leopold von Ranke (1795-1886) and Gustav Droysen (1808-1884). When history itself became the story or the text that was the object of study, it was only a small step from this vantage point to view social practices and social institutions as text analogues, the meaning of which had to be interpreted.

Hermeneutic is considered as the third phase in the evolution of phenomenology, profoundly influenced by Heidegger's works, and prominently represented by the writings of Hans-Georg Gadamer and Paul Ricoeur. This preserves the idea of the priority of being, but sees language as the all-important medium in which human being is constituted. Language is necessarily intersubjective, and precedes the consciousness of any individual, since it is the very condition of that consciousness. In this version, phenomenology comes much more immediately into contact with the social sciences, since language is recognized as an intrinsically social phenomenon whose characteristics infuse and mould the experiences of the individual. There is a major point of contact here between hermeneutic phenomenology and the philosophy of the later Wittgenstein, which also holds that language is first of all the property of a social community, and that language and the conduct of day-to-day social life are intimately intertwined (Giddens 1981: 142).

Hans-Georg Gadamer (1900-2002): Conception of Understanding

In his *Truth and Method*, published in 1985, Hans-Georg Gadamer argued that if one were to take seriously the claim of understanding being a category of life, then one could not see hermeneutics narrowly as a methodological tool, but one had to instead speak of "universal" hermeneutics, since all human experience has a hermeneutic dimension. In an unselfconscious manner, we are engaged in the hermeneutic task of understanding all the time, but we only become conscious of it when we have an experience of misunderstanding, when we feel that we have not read the situation correctly. Just as breathing is a constant part of us as long as we live, so does 'understanding' a part of our being in the world. Gadamer categorically stated that the hermeneutics he was developing was not a methodology of the human sciences. The philosophical questions of *Truth and Method* were: "what is understanding, and how is understanding possible?" Gadamer defined hermeneutics as the "basic being-in-motion of There-being which constitutes its finiteness and historicity and hence includes the whole of its experience of the world...The study of hermeneutics is thus the study of Being, and, ultimately, the study of language, because Being that can be understood is language" (as quoted in Hekman 1986: 94).

Gadamer criticised both the Enlightenment and the Romantic conception of understanding as being based on a false opposition between reason and tradition, or between judgment and prejudice. Understanding is not a matter of judgments alone; nor do prejudices always lead to misunderstanding. Similarly, if the canons of rationality enable one to understand only to make sense in the context of certain traditions, then the tradition is not a matter of simple inertia. Instead, it is "constantly an element of freedom and of history itself. Even the most genuine and solid tradition does not persist by nature because of the inertia of what once existed. It needs to be affirmed, embraced, and cultivated. It is, essentially, preservation, such as is active in all historical change. But preservation is an act of reason..... At any rate, preservation is as much a freely chosen action as revolution and renewal" (Gadamer 1975).

In his thinking about hermeneutics, Gadamer, much more than Dilthey and Schleiermacher, also problematized the position of the investigator. For Gadamer, 'any interpretations of the past, whether by a historian, philosopher or linguist, are as much a creature of the interpreter's own time and place as the phenomenon under investigation was of its own period in history. The interpreters are always guided in their understanding of the past by their own particular set of prejudices. He added that the acts of understanding or interpretation require the overcoming of the strangeness of the phenomenon to be understood and its transformation into an object of familiarity in which the horizon of the historical phenomenon and that of the interpreter become united.' This fusion of horizons between the object and subject of study is possible because the historical object and the hermeneutic operation of the interpreter are both part of the overriding historical and cultural tradition or continuum, which Gadamer calls effective history.

Jurgen Habermas (1929-): The Hermeneutics of Suspicion

Jurgen Habermas methodological principles clearly showed the influence of both Marxist and Freudian theory as he was closely associated the Frankfurt school. For Habermas, the history of the human sciences shows that human beings pursued knowledge in order to fulfill three interests, namely, firstly, the knowledge constitutive interest of the empirical-analytic sciences is in technical control; secondly, the knowledge constitutive interest of the cultural sciences is practical; and thirdly, the knowledge constitutive interest of the critical sciences is in emancipation.

Positing a relation between the logical-methodological rules of a science and its knowledge constitutive interests, Habermas argued that the methodological structure of Freudian psychoanalysis is paradigmatic for a critical science of society. Habermas calls the method of psychoanalysis a form of 'depth hermeneutics' which incorporates explanation and understanding into a science oriented towards methodological self-reflection. He stated that successful psychoanalytic practice is defined in terms of the patient himself or herself being able to understand and overcome his or her neurosis; and this idea can be generalized to the position that human beings, unlike objects in nature, have a consciousness and an understanding of what it is that they are doing. He opined, 'if the social scientist does not want to stay limited to this understanding, she or he is also not to ignore it by calling it false consciousness.'

Habermas uses his category of depth hermeneutics to contest Gadamer's concept of philosophical or universal hermeneutics. He favoured that understanding the meaning of something that seems unfamiliar can come about when that unfamiliar action is placed in its historical and social context. But in the case of what he called 'systematically distorted communication', he pointed to the problem of lack of understanding which remains even when the action is contextualized. He put forward the example of a neurosis; say the compulsive washing of hands, to explain his concept. He stated, if we seek to understand the meaning of someone constantly washing hands, over and above the placing of that someone in her or his social horizon, we need to also unearth the event which triggered that neurosis in the person. In order to understand this case, we have to first explain it. Explaining his concept of 'explanatory understanding,' he said,

> "The What, the meaningful content of the systematically distorted expression, cannot be "understood" if the Why, the origin of the symptomatic scene in the conditions responsible for the systematic distortion itself, cannot be "explained" at the same time... explanatory understanding, as a depth-hermeneutical deciphering of specifically inaccessible expressions, presupposes not only, as simple hermeneutical understanding does, the trained application of naturally acquired communicative competence, but a theory of communicative competence as well. Such a theory concerns itself with the forms of the inter-subjectivity of language and the causes of their deformation" (1985: 305).

Wanting to employ depth hermeneutics as a resource for the emancipatory interest of the critical sciences, Habermas asks us to be conscious of the problem of the understanding turning into reconciliation in Gadamerian hermeneutics. Unless we are conscious of the possibility of 'systematic distortions,' he added, the 'strangeness of the phenomenon' might be overcome not through explanatory understanding but through reconciliation.

Paul Ricoeur (1913-2005)

In his 'The Model of the Text' (1973), in order to prove the relevance of hermeneutics as a method to the social sciences, Ricoeur highlighted, 'human action as having the same structure as a written text.' He distinguished between spoken and written discourse. In written discourse, unlike in an oral conversation, the link between the author and the meaning of what the author has written, as well as the link between the meaning of what is written and the specific interlocutor to whom it is addressed, is broken. Like written discourse, human action is also detachable from its author; it has consequences of its own, it always goes beyond its relevance to its initial situation, and it can be seen as addressed to an infinite number. He emphasized that 'these various similarities are sufficient to warrant the treatment of action as a text and so to justify the distinctive status of a hermeneutical discourse on human action' (1973: 91-117).

Like Habermas, Ricoeur also sees psychoanalysis as a type of hermeneutics. But this hermeneutics, Ricoeur pointed out, is not a hermeneutics of faith; it is, rather, a hermeneutics of suspicion. Whereas the hermeneutics of faith is animated by a willingness to listen and by a respect for the object as a revelation of the sacred, the hermeneutics of suspicion is animated by a skepticism towards the given and a rejection of respect for the object.

It is not only psychoanalysis that questions the authority of the meaning producing subject, so does structuralism: the objective meaning of a text is something other than the subjective intention of the author, and so the problem of the right understanding can no longer be solved by a simple return to the alleged intention of the author. Not that hermeneutics, even in the hands of Schleiermacher and Dilthey, ever reduced meaning to intentionality, but what is new in Ricoeur is that he begins to speak of the transition 'from Understanding to Explanation' and 'from Explanation to Understanding'. Ricoeur argued that we should consider structural analysis to be a necessary stage between a 'naïve' interpretation and a 'critical' interpretation, between a 'surface' interpretation and a 'depth' interpretation. The final movement in the dialectic of interpretation, he concluded, thus, culminates in an act of understanding that is mediated by the explanatory procedures of structuralist analysis.

13

Symbolic Interactionism

The term symbolic interactionism was coined by Herbert Blumer in 1937, in an article entitled "Social Psychology," to denote the approach represented by such thinkers as Charles H. Cooley, W.I. Thomas, Robert E. Park, E.W. Burgess, Florian Znaniecki, William James, John Dewey, and George Herbert Mead (1962: 153). In a later essay, "Society and Symbolic Interaction," Blumer argues that Mead, more than any of the others, laid out the main premises of this approach, though he did not "develop its methodological implications for sociological study" (1962: 180). The perspective developed largely at the University of Chicago, and it was Blumer, his colleagues and students who evolved its main outline in a series of empirical, theoretical and methodological studies published between 1930 and 1950. Despite its being overshadowed by structural functionalism during the 1950s and early 1960s, this "immensely productive variant of interpretative sociology" experienced a major resurgence since 1970s.

Symbolic interactionism refers both to a set of ontological assumptions concerning the nature of social life and a set of methodological prescriptions which, it is claimed, are consistent with the perspective's ontology. Blumer writes, symbolic interaction "refers to the peculiar and distinctive character of interaction as it takes place between human beings." Actors do not simply react to each other but interpret and define each other's' actions. An actor's response is not immediate and direct but rather based on an assessment of the meaning of the act. Human interaction is therefore mediated by the use of symbols, "by interpretation or by ascertaining the meaning of another's actions" (1962: 180).

The social metaphysics of symbolic interactionism rest on three basic premises which have been outlined by Blumer: first, 'that human beings act toward things on the basis of the meanings that the things have for them,' second, 'that the meaning of such things is derived from, or arises out of, the social interaction that one has with one's fellows,' and third, 'that these meanings are handled in, and modified through an interpretative process used by the person in dealing with the things he encounters.' These simple premises provide a view of individuals, of social interaction and of social structure which is wholly distinctive, that is to say, the social actor is seen as an active agent in the construction and interpretation of social situations and their meanings; social interaction is understood as the dynamic interpenetration of lines of action undertaken by individuals in pursuance of chosen goals, these lines themselves constituting selections from a wide variety of available roles; social structure is portrayed as dynamic processual and emergent so that its description at any single point in time is best understood as a snapshot taken of a constantly changing scene (Williams 1981: 225). Blumer wrote,

> "That human society is made up of individuals who have selves (that is, make indications to themselves); that individual action is a construction and not a release, being built up by the individual through noting and interpreting features of the situations in which he acts; that group or collective action consists of the aligning of individual actions, brought about by the individual's interpreting or taking into account each other's actions" (1962: 184).

Blumer then goes on to other premises, stated,

> "The human being has a "self," that is, he can make himself the object of his own actions, or act toward himself as he might act toward others. This enables the individual to make indications to himself, and these self-indications are what we call consciousness. Anything the individual is conscious of, ranging from the ticking of a clock to an abstruse meaning is a self-indication, and the conscious life of the human-being is a steady flow of such self-indications. Further, the self and its constitution mediated by language enables the human being to abstract something from his

> surroundings, and to give it meaning to "make it into an object" (1962: 182).

The object is no mere stimulus but is constituted by the individual's disposition to act. In these terms, humans tend to construct and reconstruct their actions and hence their world.

Symbolic interaction, Blumer argued, is opposed to positing "factors" or "forces" and explaining human conduct in those terms. Even when such forces are lodged in the "social system," "social structure," etc., this procedure is opposed by symbolic interactionists because it treats individuals as "media through which such factors operate" and denies or ignores that it is individuals who act "by making indications to themselves" (1962: 185). Similarly, symbolic interaction, he put forward, opposes psychological factors and forces: "the "self" is not brought into the picture by introducing such items as organic drives, motives, attitudes, feelings, internalized social factors, or psychological components. Such psychological factors have the same status as the social factors mentioned: they are regarded as factors which play on the individual to produce his action. They do not constitute the process of self-indication" (1962: 185).

This brief summary should be sufficient to show how Blumer, in his effort to avoid the reification of dimensions of human interaction, presents us with a philosophical conception that flattens out both "society" and the "individual." On the one hand he insists on a society without structure: human society refers to the "emipirically observable activity" of acting units, whether individuals or groups, and therefore one cannot speak of "units that do not act - for example, "social classes in modern society" (1962: 187). On the other hand, he insists on individuals without organic drives.

This is a conception of reality that carries with it an ironic epistemological twist. For if we take this argument literally in its refusal to speak about "units that do not act," it becomes a crude positivism or empiricism for which the only reality is the immediately observable. If one accepts this view, one has no right to employ concepts that have no direct empirical referent. How can one speak of "social classes" if one cannot observe their acting? At the same time Blumer's fear of reification leads him to deny drives, motives, attitudes, and feelings to deny everything but the "self" indicating itself, whether alone or in alignment with other such self- or other-indicating selves. "Society" is thus nothing more than a plurality of disembodicd selves interacting in structureless situations (Zeitlin: 1987: 216).

Methodologically, symbolic interactionists have tended towards a naturalistic perspective, stressing the necessity for studies of *real* social situations rather than the construction of artificial ones via the use of experimental designs or survey studies. In place of formal methods of data collection and analysis, they have substituted only broad and general methodological injunctions which call for an attitude of 'respect' for the phenomena under investigation. Blumer has claimed that such studies are, or at any rate should be, carried out in two stages. The first is that of 'exploration', in which the investigator's main concern is to gain first hand acquaintance with the social situations that he wishes to study, and at this stage the aim is to depict that world as it is understood and oriented to by those who live in it. Such descriptions are then likely to be uninformed by sociological theory and largely couched in participants' language. In the second stage, however, that of 'inspection', the researcher concentrates on 'analytic elements' in the setting, which are of course only available through theoretically informed observation, and for most interactionists, this stage has consisted in the identification, description and explanation of basic social processes, for example, socialization, integration, negotiation. This latter concern has often resulted in a fairly formalistic sociology, although on the part of Blumer and his colleagues there has always existed an attempt to temper this tendency with the reminder that these forms themselves only arise from the activities of human agents in pursuit of pragmatic interests (Williams 1981: 225).

Blumer explained that what is most important is to "catch" the interpretive process of interaction "as it occurs in the experience of the acting unit which uses it' (1962: 188), and above all to avoid viewing "human society in terms of structure or organization" and treating "social action as an expression of such structure or organization" (1962: 189). The desire to avoid the reification of concepts is noteworthy. Nonetheless, the use of concepts should not be confused with their reification, What epistemological principle gives one the right, let us ask, to employ the concept of "self" and to deny to others the use of the concept "social class," "impulse," etc.? Is the concept "self" more empirically verifiable than the concept "social class"? (Zeitlin: 1987: 217). It is one thing to say that "organizations and changes in it are the product of the activity of acting units and not of 'forces' which leave such acting units out of account" (1962: 189). The first part of the proposition, through the word "forces," is a fruitful reminder that only individuals act, not organizations or "forces" however, the remainder of the sentence simply calls attention to a mystical reification of "forces" in an organizational context or to bad sociology, or to both. Only those sociologists who do in fact posit "forces" in society independent of acting individuals have need for Blumer's methodological injunction.

But Blumer appears to want to rule out the possibility of speaking of social organization and "forces" even when one does in fact take account of the acting individuals. What else can it mean to say that "the organization of a human society is the framework inside of which social action takes place and is not the determinant of that action" (1962: 189). If we take this at face value it is either meaningless or false. Are the relationships, formal or informal, in terms of which men interact, merely impotent frameworks? If some men control property and other resources while other men do not, and the latter are able to earn their livelihood only by working for the former, would Blumer deny that this relationship is a determinant of action? If those who are high in a bureaucratic hierarchy command while those who are low obey, is that organization a "mere" framework, or a determinant of action? Is prison a mere framework? school? family?

If Blumer meant to indicate by this infelicitous formulation that individuals are not totally or passively shaped by their participation in organizations or position in formal relationships, then he would be pointing to an important truth. It is apparent, however, that Blumer intends more than this for he has a definite theory about society: "In the case of human societies, particularly modern societies, in which streams of new situations arise and old situations become unstable, the influence of organization decreases" (1962: 190). Modern society is an increasingly classless, structureless, "criss-crossing of lines of action...in which the actions of participants are not previously regularized and standardized" (Ibid.).

Here Blumer has abandoned Mead's dialectical philosophy and has presented in its place a one-sided interpretation that denies altogether social relationships, social structure, and social organization. Society, from this standpoint, becomes a plurality of disembodied, unconstrained selves floating about in amorphous situations. Little wonder that this perspective has been dubbed "symbolic interaction" (Zeitlin: 1987: 218).

By and large Blumer's conception, not Mead's, has prevailed and dominates symbolic-interactionist thinking and research today. We cannot begin to review the work of the numerous adherents of his "school" here. There are now available, in any case, several collections of representative writings. A quick glance at any one of the most recent of these collections will reveal the way in which contemporary adherents have centered on one dimension of Mead's conception to the virtual exclusion of all others, treating social interaction and socialization as if these processes were nothing more than symbolic communication. Society is dissolved into discourse. The fact that language is essential to man apparently is taken to mean that human interaction and socialization can be understood as if they were symbolic processes and nothing more.

14

Feminism

The sociology of knowledge presumes that knowledge, much like social institutions and beliefs, is socially constructed and therefore has a necessary symbiotic relationship with social classes, castes, groups and communities. However, while it is easy to discern the domain assumptions that characterise those systems of knowledge, which are marginal and seen as overtly political, the same is not true of established dominant approaches. Hence it is only with the surge of post-colonial writings that it now may appear that Orientalism or a west centricity marked the classical comparative approaches. Unlike this apparent neutrality that shrouded the comparative method, the feminist method is seen as overtly political. Indeed a false but persistent dichotomy is created between the academic and political approaches. In the case of the feminist method, however the hostility often is intense and responses range from a tendency to trivialise to a tendency to demonise. Such responses can be understood in the context of the far-reaching and fundamental challenges that the feminist method poses to conventional knowledge systems.

Despite various feminist movements, formal equality for women took long to come. The suffragette movement of the West was a long-drawn out struggle. Women in late nineteenth century England were not recognised as individuals in either the legal or liberal theoretical sense. Men still had formal power over the rest of the family and women were mostly excluded from the public sphere. Mill and Taylor, along with some early United States feminists such as Elizabeth Cady Stanton and Susan B. Anthony, argued that the equality of women required full citizenship for women. This would include giving women enfranchisement. After 1865, when Mill was in the English parliament, he fought for women's suffrage. He also fought "to amend the laws that gave husbands control over their wives' money and property" (Eisenstein 1979: 128).

Furthermore by the 1980s, it was becoming clear that the feminist scientific revolution, like those that Kuhn (1970) had studied, would not take place without resistance. As Kuhn has noted, scientific disciplines are aptly named; they discipline thought by making some ideas seem natural and others almost unthinkable. The practice of science involves commitments to such disciplines. The commitments of the scholarly community to certain ideas and ways of thinking seem to stand in the way of new theories, however useful they might prove to be in the long run. While calling for a critical appraisal of research in women's studies Krishnaraj said, "Feminist research is expected to use theory not so much to test hypotheses but develop a better understanding through grounded concepts" (2005: 2008-2017).

Feminist method helps us to look at the social world through the prism of gender. It intersects with other hierarchies and social forms. It is true that the classical social theorists generally excluded consideration of actions of women. Marx, Durkheim and Weber made stray comments on women and family. Generally, they focused on differences and inequality. Marx was most explicit in this, but Durkheim and Weber developed various ways of examining difference and inequality. The concepts, namely, the division of labour, exploitation and power, domination, and authority emphasized difference and inequality. Yet male and female inequalities, or racial and ethnic inequalities, form little part of classical sociology. Feminists have identified patriarchy as a social system of inequality, but classical sociology had only a limited analysis of this. Marx and Engels did have a model of male and female inequality, but it derived from property and economic considerations. Weber analysed patriarchy, but male and female inequalities were not his primary concern in such analysis. It is not surprising that Talcott Parsons' model of the family assumed women to perform expressive roles and men instrumental ones. The point in contention is not that it does not conform to the empirical reality but that it takes the extant as given, and not problematic. The traditional and modern patriarchal norms are thus embedded in the dominant theoretical formulations. The dominance of the established methods was such that it appeared to be naturalised (Harding 1987: 2-14).

While there are certainly some common features within the vast body of studies that warrant it being called feminist, it is important to assert that important differences also characterise what can be broadly termed the feminist method. A useful way to mark the growth of a feminist approach to sociological research is to identify three stages in the study of gender related issues since 1970. Initially, the emphasis was on sex differences and the extent to which such differences might be based in biological properties of individuals. In the second stage, the focus shifted to individual-level sex roles and socialisation, exposing gender as the product of specific social arrangements, although still conceptualising it as an individual trait. And, finally, the hallmark of the third stage is the recognition of the centrality of gender as an organising principle in all social systems, including work, politics, everyday interaction, families, economic development, law, education, and a host of other social domains. As our understanding of gender has become more social, so has our awareness that gender is experienced and organised in race- and class-specific ways.

It has already been emphasised that important differences exist between different feminist approaches. To start with, we can clearly distinguish between the traditional sociological approach to gender and the feminist approach. Most introductory sociology textbooks still treat gender as an individual attribute and gender inequality as an outcome of childhood socialisation. In contrast, current feminist thinking stresses the far greater input of the division of labour, power, social control, violence, and ideology as structural and interactional bases of inequality, not only between women and men, but among women and men of diverse social classes and racial ethnic groups. Maria Mies (1931-), who had in the nineteen seventies provided methodological guidelines for feminist research, stressed the need for replacing the practice of value-free research with a conscious bias towards women's struggles for social change. She also made a case for conscientisation of the researcher as well as the researched (Gorelick (1991: 461).

Methodologically, the basic premise of feminist approach to sociological research is based on the arguments which include: first, it argued that research designs were based on men's experiences; second, it argued against a separation and reification of a division between the public and private; thirdly, it recognised the diversity of gender statuses in the social order; and, fourthly, it argued for reflexive sociological inquiry. Feminist social scientists demanded a fundamental transformation in how questions are asked and what criteria are employed to define an answer as acceptable. Illustrative of this is the long practice of assuming that the head of the household is the eldest male member. It has been increasingly shown that the number of female headed households in the rural areas of India is very high. But the very, concept of a head of household was based on the urban middle class men's experience that women are 'housewives'. Another very common example is the manner that the category 'work' assumed that it meant ' regular work outside the home for which wages were given. However it has been increasingly realised that women for the most part work in the informal sector, in what are termed as household production units. Instances in the city of Delhi would be bangle and toy making, zardozi, assembling of electronic parts that are subcontracted to poor women in the slums, domestic workers etc. Indeed concerted efforts were made in the 1991 census to educate both census personnel and ordinary citizens that breaking stones or carrying bricks is also work. Apart from this informal work, which is growing with globalisation, the idea that housework is also 'work' is still considered alien.

The feminist method is against a separation and reification of a division between the public and private. In sociological research, when gender was seen primarily as an organising principle of the family, the other areas of social life were falsely conceptualised as "ungendered." The division between an ungendered "public" sphere and a gendered "private" sphere is both ideological and misleading. One aspect of the long history of modern, urban, industrial society was the development of a separation between the public and private spheres. These had not always been separated in traditional societies, although there was often a sex-based division of labour and male dominance. But there is no doubt that with the development of capitalism, cities and industry, a public sphere dominated by men and male activities developed. Women generally became restricted to the private sphere of household and family, and had limited involvement in political, economic, or even social public life. While women were involved in more public activities, there were movements to restrict the participation of women in public life, for example, factory legislation and the family wage. Illustrative of this would be the fact that male professionals would be preferred in the corporate sector and the argument given would be that men are more committed to work while women would be distracted; they get married and pregnant. The significant point is that men to get married and become fathers but the dominant assumption is that the private sphere comprises the cleaning, cooking, shopping, child care, attending parent-teachers meet, looking after the sick, would be the women's work. The public sphere of work for women cannot therefore be reorganised until the private sphere is. In developing countries and increasingly in the developed ones too there are part-time or full-time female domestic workers. Sri Lankan, Philippino and Bangladeshi women among others are migrating across national borders to run middle class homes. This leads us to the third point about the intersection of gender with other categories like class or ethnicity.

In the twenty-first century, the sociological research has carried forward the 'reflexive' stance. The transformations we seek in the disciplines are also transformations of our own ways of thinking. It is useful and reassuring then, to share with others that the 'actual expertise and language of women is the central agenda for feminist social science and scholarship' (Du Bois 1983: 108). Feminist researchers have over the last decade been increasingly emphasising the need to hear the voices of women. Engendering sociological inquiry means interrogating the processes by which sociological discourse was gendered by putting forth feminist reflexive understanding of sociology as emancipatory. As Rege said, "The uphill task is of reconceptualising basic categories of analysis, once the experiences of the marginalised have been brought to centre" (2003: 41). Furthermore, the feminist approach works to make gender visible in social phenomena, asking if, how, and why social processes, standards, and opportunities differ systematically for women and men. This approach also recognizes that gender inequality is inextricably entwined with other systems of inequality. Looking at the world through a gender lens thus implies two seemingly contradictory tasks. First, it means unpacking the taken for granted assumptions about gender that pervade sociological research, and social life more generally. At the same time, looking through a gender lens means showing just how central assumptions about gender continue to be the organisation of the social world regardless of their empirical reality (Ferree 1999: xii).

The study of gender occupies now a significant space in sociological research. The contribution of the feminist approach to social research is not confined to providing narratives of women's experiences and to highlight the signs of sexism in conventional sociology. The feminist approach has contributed the inclusion of new themes and concepts and has now grown quite sensitive to its critics and as a result it tends today to be more inclusive. It is inclusive in the sense of focusing on more diverse experiences and perspectives of women of different races, ages, colours, cultures and histories; and pays attention to contexts rather than predefined, operationalized hypotheses. This trend has meant useful analyses of gender relations, which are increasingly correlated with the issues of racism, ethnocentrism and socio-economic formations. Feminism is no more a fad and the feminist approach is reflective of larger transformations in the perceptions and constructions of social reality. Almost all over the world, there is a conscious effort in higher education institutions to integrate theory and research on gender in the curricula as a whole. This indicates the currents of transformation in the disciplines of social sciences. Instead of arguing for a separate feminist methodology, the attempts are made to locate feminist research within the theoretical and methodological discourse in mainstream social sciences.

Feminist Discourse in India

The feminist discourse in India has organised itself around its critique of marriage and family. In this context, it may be said that the feminists in India have articulated the debate in the last three decades of the twentieth century by theorising not only around deconstruction of oppression of women but also its negotiation and transformation in real life situations. Focussing on the economic class aspects of women's oppression, socialist feminism has engaged in discussing the relationship between sexual, economic class and racial oppression. Scholars, like Hensman (2005: 709), have provided a socialist feminist critique of marriage, family and community as they feel that 'the original left critique is inadequate.' Similarly, John (2005: 712) has studied family and marriage in a historical perspective and shown how the social reform movement "during the nineteenth and early twentieth century engaged with the domestic domain via a critique of 'tradition', as embodied by specific subjects such as widows, child brides and others." Not just confined to the upper and middle class social reality, the feminists in India have drawn our attention to emerging critiques by Dalit and lower caste women. Formation of an all India group by the name of National Federation of Dalit Women symbolised another arena of debate around caste-based inequalities and Indian feminists faced the challenges that this critique brought out into the open about the invisibility of Dalit women's perception of exclusion from the mainstream the feminist movement. Violence against women and legal inequalities were of course the key themes discussed extensively by feminists in India but now they are entering the domain of marriage and family in the light of now fairly common occurrences, clashes of perceptions about sexuality and gender relationships.

Part IV

Methodological Guidelines for Social Research

15

Observation and Logic in Social Research

The art of observation and logical understanding of social reality have remained central methodological concern for social scientists, especially for those who had as their objective the study of society, as against the study of individuals, as in psychology. As discussed earlier, the tussle for primacy between empiricism and logic have been resolved in the social sciences by the need for both to come to a conclusion regarding social reality. The two ways of understanding social reality are known as the deductive and the inductive methods. The deductive method takes a few axioms or so-called true statements with the aim of proving other true statements or theorems, which logically emanate from them. In this method, logic is the main operating tool. If a statement emanates logically from the axioms, it must be true. The inductive method, on the other hand, makes many observations about nature, with the aim of discovering a few but strong statements about how nature works or about what are the laws and theories that are at the back of how nature appears to us. In this method (often called the scientific method), observation of nature is the main operating tool. If an idea is in conflict with what occurs in nature, the idea has to be given up as useless. By now most social scientists agree that the processes of inductive and deductive reasoning run simultaneously. As one attempts to make sense of what is observed empirically, one has to rely on logic for interpretations. And again logic cannot be applied in a vacuum, it needs some kind of a solid referendum; even the imagination has its limits and cannot go beyond the frontiers of human comprehension that is ultimately linked to what can be humanly observed.

It is obvious that unlike the observations conducted in the natural sciences that depend only on the senses of the observer, the observations in social sciences need the participation of the observed. In social research, while one can rely on the senses to see what is happening, one needs to inquire from the actors as to what is the meaning of their acts for any explanation to take place. Take for example the utter bewilderment a complete outsider would face if taken to witness a football match. The meaningless actions of adult men hitting a round object and running around for no practical purpose and, worse, thousands of spectators getting so emotionally charged at the sight of such meaningless acts, would not appear reasonable to any outside and objective observer. The observer may put forward the verdict of collective insanity if not made familiar with the meaning systems that prompt the actions as well as a large amount of conceptual data as to: What is a game? Why is it played? What is the relationship between a game and national pride? So it is with every act of observation of society that we need to refer to more generalized concepts and also meaning systems of the actors. This is not to say that one relies only on explanations given by the actors but true explanation in the social sciences would then contextualize the observations, the meanings and the actor's frame of reference to a larger and more generalized system of concepts and relationships, to try to get at a true meaning, truth or explanation. Thus inductive data is contextualized by a logical process or deduction.

For the social scientists, what constitutes data when the objects of study comprise society and culture? As is evident, the nature of the data is itself sufficiently different from the data of natural sciences, as whatever we observe is a construct. Like when we observe a football match, the term "game" is a construct and unless we use this construct to explain whatever we are seeing physically, the entire observation would become meaningless. Thus, there is only one way, as argued by Dan Sperber (1982), to describe cultural and social phenomena, and that is by interpretation. But even before we go into the process of interpretation; we must be clear about what it is that we are going to interpret, that is, what is the nature of observation on which we rely as our base data.

To begin with, social scientists interpreted data or basic observations made by anyone. In the eighteenth and nineteenth centuries, travellers, missionaries and administrators collected large parts of data used. It is true that some of it still forms the basis of much of social theory, especially those accounts that could never be repeated, as the situations, societies and cultures depicted in them have since disappeared. In the nineteenth century, the prevalence was on a pure scientific methodology or on nomothetic generalizations. According to Windelband, all explanations are of two types, nomothetic and ideographic. The former refers to generalized laws and the latter to individual facts. We may for example call the laws of evolution nomothetic and the specific events of history ideographic. Since social science is deemed to be a science of society, it aspires to be nomothetic rather than ideographic.

Thus, the effort of the classical social theorists was to find the laws of societal evolution, that is, social physics, based on the assumption that society too has an objective existence like all natural objects and like all natural objects it too follows same laws or principles. The assumption of society as a natural phenomenon following laws of nature was to dissociate it from its earlier conceptualization as a divine entity following supernatural dictates. To make society, however, an object capable of being subjected to scientific analysis another criterion that had to be fulfilled includes ethical neutrality. Society and its norms had for long been entrenched within religion and cosmology so that most rules of society were viewed as divinely sanctioned rather than as a creation of humans; like incest taboos, norms of femininity and masculinity, etc. A science of society has to proceed from the premise that all such rules and norms are variable and human-made and therefore a science of society has to follow some principles of causality rather than of divine sanction. In other words, all aspects of society have a purposive existence that can be explained rationally. As Turner (2000) pointed out that study of society uses, on the one hand, formal theory, with assumptions, concepts, propositions and laws and in this sense is similar to natural science, and as such it explores empirical data, practices and institutions and tries to find causal and generalizing statements. This approach finds its proponents in the writings of Hempel (1942), Rudner (1966), Braybrooke (1987), Kincaid (1990), McIntyre Lee (1991), etc. On the other hand, for many social scientists, namely, McIntyre Alisdair (1973), Turner (1974), Sahlins (1976), Geertz (1983), etc. it is not possible to develop generalizing and causal explanations due to the diversity and multiplicity of the social world. They argued that social scientists' focus on observation of local action and interaction helps it to develop analyses of various social contexts. In fact, as observed by Turner, "social theory thrives and survives best when it is engaged with empirical research and/or public issues" (2000: 12). As a matter of fact, even social scientists in the nineteenth century were linked to a critical agenda toward the then social reality, as Barnes remarked, Auguste Comte was linked to "programmes of political action" (1977: 42).

Therefore, for logical understanding of social reality, the emphasis should be on relevant empirical sources of data, on the demarcation between observation and theory, and on logical consistency and deductive coverage. Furthermore, for scientific inquiry into social reality, as pointed out by Elster (1989) and Little (1991), sociological research needs to discover regularities derived from underlying causal properties of social phenomena. Also, it is not necessary for us to draw an analogy between social sciences and natural sciences in order to stress the explanatory significance of discovering regularities in the social world. It is by now explicitly understood that the social sciences cannot emulate the way natural scientists derive laws from the properties of physical phenomena. In other words, social sciences do not require scientific explanation in terms of law-like regularities. Nevertheless, causal hypotheses confirmed by empirical data are parts and parcels of social science research. But, then, methodologically, sociological research offers weak generalizations which have only tentative predictability.

So, the question arises: what kind of generalizations or regularities we have in social research? Broadly speaking, there are two types of regularities, namely, governing regularity and phenomenal regularity. The former is linked to law of nature, that is, as per a particular law of nature, there will always be generation of a particular kind of behaviour. For example, it is a governing regularity that forces of electrodynamics affect protons and electrons. On the other hand, the latter is linked to common features of social entities and their effects on individual agency. It has been observed, for example, that land-tenure systems with a particular structure create common incentives for individuals wherever they are implemented; it is then a regularity of these systems that they have common features, for example, under investment in capital improvements. But these regularities are strictly derivative from features of individual agency, and they do not represent governing regularities of a certain kind of social institution (Little 1992: 6). To elaborate, since social reality is highly diverse, and constantly experiencing cross cutting varieties of causation, it is possible only to produce scientifically valid knowledge in terms of "exception-laden phenomenal regularities" and "the highly qualified regularities that derive from institutional logic analyses" (Little 1992: 20). Thus, in methodological terms, in the social sciences we need to be aware of the scope and limits of generalizations possible in the light of the nature of our subject matter.

16

Rules of Data Collection

As far as collection of data is concerned, the major question is how to exercise the use of the sensory with the caution that no ideas should be formed independent of the sensory perceptions. The data collection should rely on perceptions formed necessarily with reference to scientific methods of causality, that is, to look beyond individual manifestations to identify and classify phenomena. In other words, it involves the question of subjectivity, that is to say, to what extent we can remain objective as observers when something that we see evokes intense emotions in us as human beings. In the social sciences the question has still not been resolved completely but certainly many social scientists have abandoned the stand of neutrality and we may find many scholar activists who consider it ethically wrong to remain neutral and emotionless when dealing with human situations. There is a recognition among such scholars that we can set up some universal criteria such as universal concept of human rights to intervene in situations that we enter as observers. Sometimes the entry may be for the specific purpose of intervention as in development studies or when social scientists are called in as advisors and consultants. But the debate whether to intervene or not to intervene is never-ending.

As a matter of fact, the scientific approach or even the social scientists approach accepts something only by way of its inherent properties, and not by any ideas regarding it. It has been realized with respect to social data, such an observation without interpretations, or the quest for inherent properties, is an illusion. Everything about society follows a system of meaning bestowed on it by culture or by humans. For example concepts like femininity, masculinity, etc., are all parts of meaning systems. There may be many societies where such terms hold one meaning and in others they may mean quite different things. Margaret Mead (1901-1978) in her work, *Sex and Temperament in Three Primitive Societies* (1935), had undermined all notions of femininity and masculinity held as "natural" in western societies. My own class were into squeals of laughter when I described the men in their curls and make-up flirting with the plain-looking women of the Tchambuli, New Guinea. In December, 1931 Mead in her study of Tchambuli Culture travelled to New Guinea to study the Arapesh and later the Mudugumor and Tchambuli cultures. Here, her fieldwork consisted of studying sex roles in culture. Mead found that in Arapesh culture, both men and women were expected to be equal. This culture was found to be very simple as both genders actively raised the children. On the other hand, Mudugmor culture was very fierce. Both men and women were mean and aggressive. Often the children were left to fend for themselves and infants of the wrong sex were commonly cast into the river to die. This, in itself, was a very alarming experience for Margaret. In Tchambuli culture, Margaret found that the sex roles were reversed. The women were brisk and hearty and the men were in charge of the household. Whether or not Mead's descriptions were correct, they certainly dispelled the myth of "what is natural."

In social research, we may find many supporters of empiricism who follow the empirical approach without subscribing to empiricism. This means that they do not accept the theoretical premises of empiricism and do not like to support it as a doctrine. Nevertheless, they find it acceptable to follow the empirical approach as a methodology. As discussed earlier, the empirical approach refers to the methodology of collecting facts through observation and other first-hand methods of data collection. There is a difference of opinion and method in whether one relies on the data collected only by a particular method designated as "scientific" or on the data collected by any lay person. In the initial period of the growth of the social sciences, scholars such as Herbert Spencer (1820-1903), Auguste Comte (1798-1857) and even Edward Burnett Tylor (1832-1917) and Lewis Henry Morgan (1818-1881), depended largely on the data collected by travellers, missionaries and administrators passing through various territories. The emphasis at this time was on the logical process of analysis, the data served only to illustrate the ideas and fill in the schema, whose origin lay in the brains of the "armchair" scholars. The scholars relied on their own intuitive judgment to select data and to compare them. Against such practices came up the insistence on scientific collection of data, with some rules to be strictly followed if one was to claim authenticity of the facts gathered. In the field of sociological research, Durkheim (1858-1917) in his *Rules of the Sociological Method* (1964, first published in 1895) recognized that the data must be collected not just anyhow, but keeping certain rules in mind. As Durkheim perceived it, social phenomena must have an external existence and must be treated separate from the representations of them in the mind. Descartes (1596-1650), in his book *Meditations on First Philosophy* (first published in 1641; English translation published in 1991), laid the basis of the scientific method by the simple rule of doubt and advocated the strategy of beginning by doubting the truth of everything.

Three Universal Rules

First, the collection of data must be done without any subjective understanding, preconceived notions or prejudices. A truly scientific approach does not accept anything without proof and this discounts much of the second-hand data relied upon by the "armchair" scholars. Also, scientists rely on data collected explicitly for the goals of the scientific endeavour.

Second, the social scientist must remain ethically and emotionally neutral. The rule of cultural relativism is the outcome of such a mindset. For, one must accept that whatever does not belong to one's own culture is not "wrong" or "strange". The principle of getting over "ethnocentrism", or regarding only one's own conceptions and values as proper, is something that is taught to all students of the social sciences but is the most difficult to overcome.

Third, the objectivity that Durkheim had aspired to introduce into the social sciences presumed that things could be identified according to their external observable characters and that it was also possible to classify similar phenomena. A very important dimension of classifying was how one defined a certain trait or institution. Many a time a feature may remain invisible or unrecognized if one looks for superficial resemblances only. In this sense, the definition of "external visibility" is to be exercised with caution. For example, the early anthropologists could not locate anything resembling a political institution among the so-called primitive societies. But later with their seminal work, *African Political Systems*, Fortes and Evans-Pritchard (1940: 6-7) recognized the political as embedded in other social institutions, such as kinship, and they identified it not by its overt form but by its function. Durkheim undertook the analytical task of apprehending a mode of classification. In their essay, *Primitive Classification*, Durkheim and Mauss (1963; first published in 1903) distinguished symbolic classification of a moral or religious nature from practical schemes of technological distinctions (Needham 1963: xi). At the end of his Introduction to Durkheim and Mauss's essay (English translation), Needham says, "It is the cardinal achievement of Durkheim and Mauss's essay, with all its imperfections, to have conceived the analytical notion of "classification" in sociological inquiry."

Role of Intuitive Understanding

There was a presumption that we could view society as a functioning body that could be explained in terms of timeless laws like the functioning of a natural organism. The idea of "social order" was one such concept that sought to explain many things, so were the concepts of "system" and "equilibrium". The only reliable data was the one collected by trained social scientists in the field by themselves. Even for purposes of comparison, one could legitimately refer only to the work of other social scientists and not to that of the "lay person" including the historian. In addition, as more and more "observers" entered the field it became apparent that the role of the "impersonal" observer was almost a myth. The raging debate between Margaret Mead and Derek Freeman over the data of the Samoans is a case in point (Kloos 2004: 140). The entry of the Conflict theorists challenged the build-up of theory around the concepts of equilibrium and social order; and, increasingly, it was felt that the observer tends to observe according to an unconscious and simultaneous process of "internal" analysis.

The ignoring of history became an issue as it became apparent that no society is without a history. Historical documents, life histories, narratives and the verbatim statements of the observed became more and more a part of the observed data in order to overcome the subjectivity of the observer. Instead of "logic", the role of intuition became more recognized in the process of scientific observation. Commenting on intuitive understanding, Sperber (1982) said that the knowledge that is acquired in the field is brought home as loads of data, in the form of field diaries, films, recorded interviews, filled schedules, maps, historical documents, life histories, pictures and genealogies. But along with it is the intuitive understanding that a scholar acquires in this field area by his/her long exposure to a culture.

It has been recognized that to get an intuitive understanding a researcher has to spend a long time with the people or situation to be studied. By the time the work is complete, along with the factual or material data, the scholar acquires an empathetic understanding by which he/she starts to understand the world through the eyes of the people she/he has spent time with. Things that appear strange in the beginning start to fall in place. While presenting the data the social scientists then recast it in the mould of a general level of conceptual understanding shared across the discipline and tread an intermediate path between the intuitive understanding that is purely personal and the interpretation of data that presents this understanding in the form of a general conceptual framework. What remains important is that just the collection of data or mere observation does not serve the purpose of understanding. What makes the crucial difference between a good work and a mediocre one is the level of intuitive understanding that a scholar can bring to the data.

One important dimension of collection of material for analysis is that in spite of one's best efforts it is not possible to see and observe each and every thing in the field situation. Scholars who believed in the scientific and objective nature of their work, abstracted from the particular to the general, and concluded that there exists a homogeneous society. In this sense, what was being said was meant for the entire society as a whole. To a large extent such a method is followed even today but attempts are made to identify the diversities within groups and cultures. Therefore, everything that does follow a set pattern is not assumed to be deviant but diverse. A method often used, that of statistical frequency, does not always yield results that are true representations of the situation. A statistical frequency often yields only a result the causes of which have to be deciphered by more qualitative and intuitive-deductive analysis.

In most societies, no matter how small and confined, many voices exist. In day-to-day life people do not act according to already laid-down scripts. The normative is often expressed in words but not followed in deed. Even the normative is being constantly manipulated and modified as Barth (1987) has shown in his book, *Cosmologies in the Making*. A person, who has the repository of oral knowledge, has also the means to modify it. Thus oral traditions transform themselves as they pass from mouth to mouth and from generations to generations and travel across space and time. Another kind of activity of digression may be simple individual convenience or exigency. Most of us are familiar with such 'adjustments in rituals and performances of daily life and even life cycle activities like marriage. A third kind of digression may be deliberate, an act of rebellion or defiance. Such acts have been studied under the label of contra-culture and often refer to the acts of resistance of marginal groups in society like women and the underprivileged.

17

Concern with Theory in Social Research

The *Oxford Dictionary of Sociology* defined theory as "an account of the world which goes beyond what we can see and measure. It embraces a set of interrelated definitions and relationships that organizes our concepts of and understanding of the empirical world in a systematic way" (1998: 666). In this sense, we can agree with Waters (1994: 3), who put forward that social theory needs to be abstract and separable from the social practices that the theory has addressed. Such a theory needs to also focus on a specific thematic argument that runs through the set of propositions providing them coherence and force. In addition to, the theory has to be logically consistent and explanatory, that is, it needs to have a thesis about social phenomena to account for their form or existence. Furthermore, the theory is to be general enough to account for all instances of the phenomena it proposes to explain. Also, the theory cannot be reduced to the explanations informants or participants themselves provide to explain their behaviour. Finally, the theory needs to be substantively valid, that is, it is to be consistent with what is already known about the social world by its participants and by the social scientists. This means that it should be possible to link the theory to other bodies of knowledge. In other words, we can say that theory refers to knowledge arranged so that the facts are subsumed under general principles. The difference between commonsensical knowledge and scientific knowledge is that the latter is systematized and classified. But only classification does not make any knowledge scientific. While commonsensical knowledge is satisfied most often with the desired effects, science looks into the causes of a phenomenon. It is the task of theory to organize such causal relationships into observable repetitive or classifiable regularities so that one can make general observations that encompass diverse but related phenomena and explain them by not individual and specific relationships only but by a higher and abstracted general relationship. To look for causes underlying any observable phenomenon is the first task of science for otherwise as often happens with respect to commonsense, people expect or demand contradictory goals without realizing that they are doing so. Establishing the correct causal relationship between facts is followed by bringing together diverse facts within a single frame of causality; the process by which this is done is called theory building. The resulting relationship is often called a theory.

The three constituents or properties of theory are explanation, prediction and verification. The systematically interrelated sociological propositions, which hold in different contexts, comprise theories. We can put to test each of these propositions as to how well it conforms to data and how well in relation to each other the propositions account for the outcomes in a given setting. If such a prediction is possible, we can say that the result has been explained in terms of known propositions. While verifying the sociological propositions, one needs to look for a logical relationship as well as empirical relationship. Thus, explanation, predictability and verification in theory building in social research are closely interrelated elements. The sciences by definition need to be predictive on the basis of their theories. In the natural or so called 'pure' sciences, there is a set limit on the probable range of failure of predictability of a theory before it is rejected. In the social sciences, theories rarely have that capacity for predictability yet some degree of ascertaining the truth of a situation has to be assigned to any statement for it to take on the mantle of a theory.

Propositions in all sciences are always open to scrutiny and continued research in a scientific manner means that we keep testing earlier statements for their validity. This is why science is recognized as a never-ending process; and that is why in the social sciences few concepts achieve the status of universal and timeless truths as in mathematics. Statement of absolute validity, like two plus two is equal to four, is rarely possible in the social sciences. There is always recognized a difference between "theories" based on constructs and "experimental laws" based on facts. In this sense, the social sciences are by and large theoretical and not experimental. Nevertheless, we build theories in the social sciences. The question arises, why do we need theories?

What is Concepts?

It is beyond doubt that whenever we are talking in terms of theory there is a necessity to use a kind of vocabulary that is often specific to a particular discipline and contains terms that we call concepts. Concepts are basic elements of theories and we develop them through a process of definition. Theories basically connect concepts to one another in a logical manner. These concepts are nothing but short hand versions of a large range of phenomena that may be brought under single heading to describe something. Here, we can mention an example of the concept of culture. When a social scientist uses the term 'culture' in any written or oral discourse, the meaning of the term is roughly comprehensible to anyone who has knowledge of the discipline. Thus, each concept is usually accompanied by a standardized description called its definition. In the natural sciences such definitions are very precise but in the social sciences they may not be so. Anyone who has struggled with the definition of culture will know how difficult it is to find a one-line definition of culture. Even today, most scholars may not agree on any definition whatsoever. Yet most social scientists would have a fairly good idea of what is meant when the term culture is used. Therefore, all scientific disciplines have their own terminology of concepts.

It is universally accepted, although, the capacity for culture building may be a genetic mechanism, culture by itself is a learnt behaviour as proven by the example of children who have been deprived of being nurtured by human adults. This learnt behavior is transmitted over generations but is also capable of being transferred to other groups and transformed over a period of time. The traits, which often go into the definition of the concept of culture, have been abstracted from actual observations and recording of human groups and their behaviour. Also, it is quite likely that certain properties considered to be true at one point of time may be given up or modified when fresh evidence comes up. For example, the proposition that only human beings are capable of culture is being modified by fresh research on non-human species. So, it can said that the concepts are abstractions that are not made randomly but by a recording of structural properties rigorously selected from the visible traits exhibited by the phenomenon under study. Although such selection can be made on the basis of statistics, the ultimate construct is made intuitively or deductively. As far as possible it is ensured that the properties selected are of universal occurrence.

Why Do We Need Theory?

The question arises: why do we need theory in the social sciences? The reason is that theories help us to put order in a bewildering range of phenomena that might seem unrelated, that is to say, with the help of theory, we may summarize in terms of a few principles the nature of the relationship between them. Broadly speaking, the more abstract a theory, that is, the more generalized a theory, the wider is its application but the further away it is from actual situations.

There are two types of theory, namely, formal and substantive. Formal theory is most inclusive and basic in the sense that it aims to isolate a single set of principles, which are the foundation for social life. Through these principles you can explain every social phenomenon. Its paradigms give birth to grand theories. Evolutionary theory is an example of a grand theory, which makes some broad generalizations regarding the nature of society and the nature of transformations that one expects to see, but it would not be very predictive when applied to everyday realities of life except in a very broad sense. The last significant attempt to write grand theory was made by Sorokin (1962). His theory on social and cultural change attempts to establish two basic law-like generalizations (Zetterberg 1965: 15-16). As a reaction to writing grand theory, Pitrim Sorokin's student, Robert K. Merton (1968: 5-10), formulated theories of middle range. We can say that these are partial theories. Such theories endeavour to explain specific but generally branching out events or specified types of the social process. When we designate a theory partial or middle range or miniature, we mean that this theory does not contradict other accepted theories. Examples of such middle range theories are Pareto's theory of elites, Murdock's (1975) theory of kinship structures, Homan's (1950) theory of elementary social behaviour.

Finally, it has been universally recognized that, whether grand or middle range, a theory is a necessity for it simplifies the task of dealing with reality. Simmel (1858-1918) wrote, "...we shall discover the laws of social forms only by collecting such societary phenomena of the most diverse contents, and by ascertaining what is common to them in spite of their diversity" (1898: 829-836). In other words, a theory provides a means for dealing with reality in terms of providing neat and compact explanations that can be set into a known explanatory framework. Simmel's assumption is that social research can discover a small number of propositions, which would be verifiable in diverse contexts. In this sense, we can say that the task of the social theorist is to discover general propositions. Such an effort generates systematically interrelated propositions. Only after generating such propositions can we test a theory. To test a theory, we need to check how well each proposition of the theory conforms to data. Interestingly, often the situation is the other way round and most of those engaged in social research collect data and look for theories to make sense of their data. In fact, the task of collecting empirical data often culminates in the researcher trying to make sense of the data in terms of available theories. If such a task is successfully accomplished then the data stand explained. However, if the data refute or contradict the theory then they provide a basis for reformulation of the existing theory or a new theory altogether. For example neo-evolutionary theories such as that of Leslie White (1945: 339-56), (1947: 165-92) and (1959: 15-24) were modifications of the evolutionary theory. The replacement of the evolutionary theory by the functional theory was a refutation of the earlier theory and its replacement by another.

Scope of Social Science Theory

We need to consider the significant contribution of social theory to highlighting false notions dearly held by people about the social world. Such ideas often manifest themselves as prejudices and become a source of unnecessary social conflict. In other words, social research itself is often instrumental in changing human behaviour. If human beings are made aware of destructive or potentially disruptive behaviour then they can and do make conscious efforts to change it. Therefore, a social scientist has to go beyond dispelling false notions about social reality. Quite often, the social science research findings tally with commonly held views and in those cases social scientists appear to be talking rather common sense things about social reality because their findings become an integral part of the everyday stock of knowledge. We have already considered the example of the political. It can be shown that as far as the function of the political is the exercise of power or to negotiate such power differentials, it can be achieved through institutions and mechanisms that normally are identified as the family, kin relationships or religious rituals.

In this way, the subjects and objects of study in the social sciences have a dynamic interactive relationship. For example, if certain kinds of child rearing practices are shown to be harmful for the normal development of the child, then they may be arguably modified or abandoned. Any predictions made by the study on the ill-effects of a particular practice may be reversed during the course of research itself.

Nowadays a significant aspect of social research is that it is possible that subjective dimensions of human behaviour, like moods, dispositions, emotions and values are open to sensory perception and therefore, form part of externally observable data. The conclusions that we reach regarding such subjects are based either on the information given to us by the actors or by a process of empathetic understanding where the scholar tries to get into the place of the actor. Rosaldo (1984), in his article 'Grief and a Head Hunter's Rage' puts himself in the place of the head hunter to analyze the anguish that is felt at the death of a loved one, at the loss of his wife Michelle Rosaldo. Thus the social scientist interprets the actions in terms of the subjective experiences as a human being and being subject to the same emotions and motivations as any other. On the other hand it is also realized that one need not step mentally into the shoes of the actors to understand a phenomenon. For example one need not be suicidal at any point of time to do a sociological analysis of suicide. But there is certainly a qualitative difference between the kind of analysis that looks at the phenomenon from the outside and the more reflexive kind of descriptive work.

Furthermore, a lot of research in sociology and anthropology has been directed towards revealing what has been variously called latent functions or unintended consequences of human actions. However, once made public these do not remain latent or unintended and may in fact replace the earlier ways of thinking by the actors themselves. For example, in urban India marriage is by and large not considered a religious or sacred ceremony to the extent that it was believed to be a generation back. More people would point to it as an occasion to bring the family together or to cement social relationships or to increase social solidarity, a function of marriage that in the earlier times was perhaps more visible to the social analysts than to the actors themselves.

Moreover, not all types of human behaviour are subjective and there are many concrete and visible outcomes of behaviour that can be measured and studied. An alternate manner of constructing theory came from the behaviourists who rejected the vagueness implied in 'subjective' understanding. An extreme behaviourist position may deny all subjective and internal mental conditions but most prefer a modified version. Here the introspective data from subjects is treated as data and then subjected to analysis. This is similar to the approach where contradictory inputs by various actors in the field are analyzed as data that represent the conditions of the field, like different power positions occupied by the actors or conflicting identities.

Theory Building and Values of Researcher

In order to assess the value-oriented bias of social science inquiry, we need focus on entry level of the values assumed by a social scientist into the process of theory formation, that is to say, how do values held by researcher affect theory building? The four points at which values can enter is at the level of: selection of problems; determination of the contents of conclusions; identification of facts; and assessment of evidence.

Selection of problems: A researcher is influenced by several considerations in the choice of subject matter of which her/his value orientation is one, that is, a Marxist would select to work on subjects like agrarian relations or the exploitation of labour in factories, or a feminist would be interested to research women's problems. Beside this, the manner in which a concept is constructed, for example, the concept of culture or what goes into determining the status of women, is also guided by the subjective orientation of the social scientist.

Determination of contents of conclusion: The classic example of this was evident during the colonial regimes when most anthropologists took equilibrium as the natural state of societies and their theories were directed towards demonstrating how such equilibrium states are maintained. Any disruption of the equilibrium was seen as abnormal or pathological (or a condition of anomie). The value orientation of the sociologists and anthropologists colluded with that of the administrators and often both were one and the same person. Or otherwise the anthropologist was on the pay-roll of the administrator. The goal of the administrators was to establish equilibrium in their colonies. Therefore equilibrium was also the desired state and viewed as such by the scholars too. The criticism of almost all theories is based on this kind of deviation. It is felt that most social scientists have a fairly well formed idea of what is the nature of the reality that they are trying to prove and most research is aimed at proving or disproving what is already intuitively known to the researcher. Moreover, the greater interests about the society at large or moral and ethical viewpoints often creep into whatever a theory is trying to prove or disprove.

Identification of facts: It is not impossible to distinguish between facts and values and contributions to theoretical understanding may be achieved even if the values of the social scientist are at variance. For example the contribution made by avowed ideologically oriented social scientists such as Marxists is still considered of considerable theoretical significance especially if they had been able to contain their value orientations within the limits of reason.

Another remedy often resorted to in contemporary theory is to make the value orientation of any work quite clear so that the reader is not misled and is able to contextualize the theory to its orientation. This could also take care, for example, of the difficulties faced in the social sciences because of the evaluative character of the terms and concepts used. It is not always very clear as to what exactly is the distinction between facts and values. For example in the nineteen seventies a certain kind of ecological approach concentrated quite a bit on the study of resource utilization as a way of looking at a community's relationship with its habitat, often looking towards the goal of maximizing such utilization. But another school of environmentalists would vehemently be opposed to the term "resource" being used for the habitat as this term in itself is reflective of an exploitative attitude towards the environment. Such persons may not think of the environment as a resource for use by human communities but as something that has a right to existence by itself. The second point of view may look upon maximization of resource utilization as a negative rather than a positive goal. Moreover while writing ethnography one may be tempted to use words like kind or cruel, both of which cannot be understood without reference to a value framework. Contemporary ethnographies normally tend to consciously avoid using such terms preferring instead to give a detailed description of the actions leaving it to the readers to form their own judgments or using such terms by which the actors themselves designate the acts.

***The assessment of evidence*:** There is always the apprehension that not only conclusions but even the process of evaluation of data is often value loaded. Some kind of data may be totally overlooked or ignored by a social scientist simply because of innate value orientations. For example, the feminist scholars had alleged that male scholars ignored women's activities and role in society simply because of their patriarchal bias. Similarly Dalit scholars have often made allegations that upper caste scholars have often presented a biased Brahmanical view of society in India, selectively using data to do so. Even in statistical analyses, value commitments are not ruled out. But value commitments are also of two kinds, covert and overt. For example Malinowski's oversight may have been unintentional but sometimes researchers allegedly manipulate data towards a particular end. Finally, one kind of bias that is almost inevitable is the one connected with the historical and situational impact upon a student of society of the place and time to which she/he belongs. The evolution of scientific thought is also a product of the history of human society. World events and transformations of intellectual climate are determining factors that can rarely be avoided in the manner in which theory is formed.

18

How to Test Hypothesis

What a theory does is to generate a hypothesis that can be tested. A theory by itself is an abstract proposition that cannot be tested. It is also true that an only process of deduction can construct a theory, even when it is based on inductive empirical data. Consequently, the reliability of a theory lies in the testability of its hypotheses. The scepticism regarding the evolutionary theory began when it was realized that the hypothesis generated by it, such as, whether or not patriarchy precedes matriarchy, could not be proved empirically. Moreover, the methodology used for validating these hypotheses was doubted. The closer the hypothesis generated by a theory comes to the reality, the better is the theory. However, not all research is directed towards hypothesis testing, in particular, as in the social sciences there can be a descriptive research that seeks to explore hitherto unknown territories.

Furthermore, a hypothesis only posits a logical relationship between phenomena to be understood and is in itself not a description of reality, and may not correspond to every actual case on hand. For example, the hypothesis that urbanization leads to disintegration of the joint family is only a logical relationship between a particular form of family and urbanization that seeks to state that whatever urbanization stands for in terms of its very definition is antithetical to what the joint family stands for, so it is logical to presume that with greater urbanization the joint families are likely to break up. But this is not a deterministic statement about all joint families actually breaking up. It merely wishes to state the reality that whatever values or states of mind that urbanization fosters like individualism and competitiveness are at variance with the sentiments that bind families together. The hypothesis is, in this sense, a deductive statement that needs to be proved inductively. Moreover, the various ways in which theories can be constructed depends on the type of questions asked and the basic assumptions or premises that are accepted as given truths in any situation. There are also no fixed rules or methods by which one enters into a scientific investigation and often methods have to be devised according to one's requirements. For example, the scholars who developed the Culture and Personality approach had to develop their own techniques such as collection of children's drawings, recording of dreams; administration of Rorschach ink-blot tests and so on, methods that had not before been used in any sociological or anthropological fieldwork.

Therefore, we can say that for setting up hypothesis testing research we must first have a theory, because the nature of the proposed relationships is ultimately derived from theory. A theory provides the basic logic of the relationship between different phenomena. The hypotheses are generated to test the truth of these relationships and therefore the correctness of the logical process, namely, the theory that has generated them. Every hypothesis contains a statement about the relationship between at least two phenomena; one of them is the phenomenon such as female infanticide that the researcher is trying to account for. The other is one that is thought to affect or bring about the phenomenon that one is trying to account for. The first one is called the dependent variable and the second one is called an independent variable. For example, if we put forward the hypothesis that illiteracy of mother leads to female infanticide, then female infanticide is the dependent variable and the literacy level of mothers is the independent variable. To test the hypothesis one has to expose it to a situation that can show it to be false. If the hypothesis survives the effort to falsify, it then is proved true. Also, we can study the rate of female infanticide among a population of well-educated women. If the sample shows a significant rate of female infanticide that compares favourably with a corresponding sample of illiterate women, then the hypothesis is false. In other words the literacy of women is not a significant variable as far as female infanticide is concerned. If, on the other hand, the sample of educated women shows a significant drop in the incidence of female infanticide, then the hypothesis is tentatively proven. Furthermore, one could rely on statistics to provide most of the base data. But not all social science variables are measured statistically, for that one has to measure by deductive processes and set up some criteria oneself or depended upon criteria provided by other studies.

As discussed earlier, the two broad divisions of the logic of theory building in the social sciences is between those who consider the natural sciences as a model for building theory in the social sciences as well, that is to look for universal laws and invariant truths regarding society and human behaviour. The other point of view denies the possibility of ever establishing such "truth" because of the creative and diverse nature of human beings. The latter point of view supports the idea that all observations regarding society and human behaviour are contextualized in historically situated human groups and can never be universalized. However, a modification of the first point of view is that the social sciences are as precise or no precise as the natural sciences because even the propositions made by the latter often have limited application and are subject to modifications from time to time. In other words, there is an attempt to review the definition of science itself.

A number of problems may be listed to provide an answer as to why the social sciences are not capable of furnishing universal laws of the experimental type. To begin with, the first drawback of experimental approaches in the sociological research is the lack of the possibility of setting up controlled experiments to test a hypothesis. A real controlled situation is one in which the scholar can manipulate the variables at will. For the social scientists ethical and moral constraints put a restriction on such manipulations, but sometimes an attempt has been made to take ready-made situations that exhibit properties of controlled comparisons. An example of a controlled comparison is the study by Epstein (1979) of two villages in South India. The following paragraph describes how Epstein used the methodology of comparing identical situations in every respect except for one variable.

> These two villages Wangala and Datena were identical in terms of culture, social norms and structure of social relationships. Epstein's hypothesis was based upon the then popular structural-functional model that assumed interdependence between the

various parts of the social structure. It was hypothesized that the introduction of outside technology would affect the economic dimension and thus upset the earlier harmonic interdependence between the various parts of the society. The two villages selected had different technological bases, one was a dry village depending solely upon rainfall for irrigation and the other had permanent sources of water from tanks and wells. With the introduction of water from the Krishnaraj Sagar Dam built in 1931, both villages underwent changes. The wet village, Wangala, strengthened its earlier forms of social structure, by the increased cash input from better irrigation facilities and the switch over to cash cropping. The increased economic input led to a continuation of earlier structural elements like caste, performance of elaborate rituals and reinforcing of the role of caste and village panchayats. But nothing new, not even electricity, was introduced into the village. The dry village, Dalena, underwent more radical transformations in its economic roles and relationships. While it could not switch to cash cropping, people underwent transformations to non- agricultural activities. People started going to the nearby town for jobs and education and the village became structurally different from what it was before. What Epstein is able to show in her research is that the same economic change, namely irrigation from a dam, can bring about drastically different results in two villages otherwise identical but having different resource bases. The two villages are comparable because they belong to the same region; same culture and had the same type of social structure to begin with. The outside source of change is also identical; the only variable that differed was technology.

This kind of methodology with ready-made situations of comparability, where two field situations could be identified that were identical in every respect except for one variable was popular for a while. They followed what John Stuart Mill (1806-1873) had called the Method of Agreement or the Method of Differences, in which two situations were either unlike in all respects except one or were alike in all respect except one. According to Mill (1930) such situations could never occur naturally or under unmonitored conditions and since they were a necessary condition for the stipulation of general laws, the social sciences could never aspire to do so. The criticism of Mill is that even under the most stringent experimental conditions such ideal conditions may not be achieved or cannot be achieved as some variables may be related in such a manner that one will automatically change if the other is varied.

The other kind of theory building process was the use of actual experimentation in the laboratory. Such methods are often commonly used in the fields of psychology and even culture personality and socialization and child rearing studies. Experiments entail comparison of what happens in the situation of the control group with what happens in the experimental group. "Control" in this context means holding one factor constant while others vary. However the obvious drawback is that not very many social situations can be reproduced under laboratory conditions. Sometimes the changes that occur in natural conditions are of far greater magnitude than those which can be produced artificially or the emotional content is far more intense in real life than under experimental conditions. The element of play-acting may also creep into such situations. In addition, it is possible to set up field laboratories where in real-life situations one can examine variables, like in a classroom or factory.

But more often theory in the social sciences is directed towards viewing the effects of a certain phenomenon upon another or on society in general. Like a particular variable may be chosen, like dowry or building of a factory or the introduction of television into an area. Then the effects of the introduction of this variable upon the rest of society are studied. Other kinds of studies may be directed towards the cause of a certain phenomenon rather than its effects. The help of a hypothesis can set up such studies in two ways, either, where a certain relationship between the phenomenon to be studied and some other variable deemed to be causative is put forward. Or otherwise it may be a purely exploratory study where the field is being approached for the first time. The latter are often in the nature of pilot studies done prior to the setting up of a hypothesis. But they can also be full-length research of the exploratory descriptive type, for example, the *Remembered Village* by M.N. Srinivas (1976).

Three Common Methods of Testing a Hypothesis

The Pre-testing of the post-testing paradigm: It is the most common method of testing a hypothesis. The dictionary meaning of paradigm is 'example', or 'pattern'. But, in social sciences, it is "a fundamental image of the subject matter within a science. It serves to define what should be studied, what questions should be asked, how they should be asked, and what rules should be followed in interpreting the answers obtained. The paradigm is the broadest unit of consensus within a science and serves to differentiate one scientific community from another. It subsumes, defines and inter-relates the exemplars, theories, and methods and instruments that exist within it" (Ritzer 1983: 432). In this, one simply studies the field prior to the introduction of a variable and after its introduction. For example, the study of a village after the building of a road or after an event likes an election or epidemic. However, the danger of such a paradigm is that one is not sure about the variable under consideration being responsible for the transformations and there is always the problem of extraneous factors. The so-called 'before-and-after' studies are regarded as an alternative to the classical experimental design. In them, a phenomenon is studied before and after the introduction of the independent variable. A comparison of the two states will tell us about the change. F. Stuart Chapin's study (1963) of public housing in Minneapolis coined the term 'ex-post facto research' for such studies. In the Indian context, many researchers working on communities that have been displaced because of development projects (such as the construction of a dam, mining, industry) have adopted this approach.

***Static group comparison paradigm*:** Here, instead of studying the same field situation before and after, one compares two similar field situations, one with and the other without the introduction of the independent variable. For example one may have two identical neighbouring villages, but one gets access to television and the other does not. So, one may study the effects of television viewing by comparing the villages.

***Non-equivalent control group paradigm*:** In this, one compares one field situation before and after the introduction of an independent variable but also compares it with a field in which the variable has not been introduced but which is similar in all other respects. This would be the case say for example when one had two identical villages that were both studied and then one of them received a significant input, like a school. Then both schools were again studied to see what effect the school had, but now we can compare it by measuring against the village that did not receive the school. The most common source of error here would be that some sort of selection process has already taken place for the introduction of the external variable. For example, a particular population size or caste composition may be responsible for the fact that one village received a school and the other did not. To remove the possibility of such an error the field situations are chosen at random and not selectively. However, this also depends on the possibility of having such random selection, that is to say, if there are enough field situations of a similar type and whether the researcher has access to selection of any such field situation. One can have such a paradigm when the number of situations is many and equally available, say if one were to study the effects of introduction of computers in secondary schools in Delhi. The most obvious disadvantage of random sampling is that one may not get the desired result. In fact such methods are more useful for quantitative research.

Rival Hypothesis Construction

Rigidity is not a virtue because social science research of real life situations is complex and multifaceted. So, one fact that must be kept in mind while doing sociological research and using the various paradigms discussed is that as researcher one must be sensitive to the existence of alternative explanations even if one has proven the hypothesis. The process of rival hypothesis construction is a standard procedure to test the efficacy of research. The four factors that form the basis of the four major rival hypotheses are: the effects of selection, the reactive measurement effect, the effects of uncontrolled extraneous variables, and the interaction effects involving selection.

The effects of selection: A selection effect occurs whenever the treatment group or the group we are studying for the introduction of the variable is different from the comparison group because of the way in which they were selected or rejected for introduction of the particular variable, like for example school. The advantages that may be perceived as emanating from the school may be because the number of persons of a dominant caste/class is more in the particular village and the school may have been introduced because of the greater clout of the dominant caste members. So it is class advantage that may have already been there and not merely the introduction of the school that may be perceived in the study as better hygiene consciousness or better use of medical facilities, etc.

***Reactive measurement effects*:** The second rival hypothesis situation may occur when the measurement process itself may introduce transformations in the field. Like for example as it often happens when students from Delhi go to carry out field-based social research in villages, the perception of the villagers of the urban elite middle class to which the students may belong often affects the responses and sometimes even the behaviour pattern. The villagers might for example wear more urban clothes while the researchers are around or profess greater faith in modern medicine.

***The effects of uncontrolled extraneous variables*:** The third type of error is due to the introduction of uncontrolled extraneous variables, that is, those variables that were overlooked or that entered while the research was in progress.

***Interaction effects involving selection*:** The fourth type of error occurs when the selection process and extraneous variables both occur in conjunction.

Thus, hypothesis testing is a process that takes the researcher a step forward in the investigation. It is an example of the organized scepticism of science. In other words, we may say that this reflects the rejection of any statement without empirical verification. A number of works have been based on the processes of hypothesis testing and several middle range theories have emerged as a result of such inductive analysis; one good example is the work of Robert K Merton (1950) on the American Soldier, in which he had developed the theory of latent and manifest functions. The efforts to produce a rigorous theoretical analysis in the social sciences is, however, always met with scepticism as the results rarely are able to attain the status of laws but middle range theories like that of Merton, as mentioned above, can be quite effective in explaining if not predicting social behaviour.

19

Managing Diversities in Social Research

It is noteworthy to mention that we need to recognise that diversities have to be both accepted and explained in terms of the meanings they express in the data collection for social research. There is no short cut if one wants to get a real understanding of social phenomena, for all such phenomena are complex and have multiple causations and effects. Therefore, social research observations are time consuming and require painstaking sincerity in recording data. When explanations in the social sciences become problematic, one has to accept rather than ignore or reject them. In addition to, the search for a perfect explanation is also illusory; and one has to accept that human beings are creative and have freedom of expression. However, it does not mean that no regularities can be observed or no generalizations can be made. The social scientists often tread a delicate balance between regularities that are real and those that one would wish to impress upon one's data. This is the classic duality between structure and action that has to be faced in the social research. We can argue that the wider the applicability of our generalizations, the more we lose out on ground level explanations of particular events, that is to say, the general often remains an essential condition for explanation of the specific.

Furthermore, in sociological inquiry, there is still another problem that empirical observations and interpretations have to deal with. What do we do when certain things that seem to lie beyond our own sensory perceptions appear to be well within the sensory perceptions of others, or at least that is what they claim? How do we interpret it when we are told in the field by our informants that they see spirits on a regular basis or they converse with the dead as they converse with the living or that they have spouses and children in the other world with whom they communicate all the time? In order to answer these, we can discuss the example of the Saoras, a tribe of Orissa do not observe a division between the dead and the living. According to them, the dead have simply gone to live in another place, quite near to their own place of residence. They meet on a regular basis and converse. To them, this poses no problem and they often talk about a person they had met while gone to the field or to the market, but the only problem for the social scientist would be that the person is long dead. They also have their spouses and children in the spirit world with whom they keep in constant touch.

So, the question arises: how does one explain this phenomenon prevalent within the Saora tribes? If one should follow the 'scientific' rationality of relying only on one's senses then the only way to explain this would be to either say that everyone in that culture is suffering from hallucinations or is speaking lies. Another way to explain this could be that people of' different cultures have different cognitive abilities and can actually see things that we cannot. This would be something like the work of Castaneda (1971) that went beyond the credulity of many but was also accepted by many others. A third way to explain it would be that there are culturally learnt mechanisms of deriving meanings from some optical and other sensory perceptions that elude us. For example, in the mountain community when a person was about to die, a lama was called in to observe the passage of escape of the soul from the body. When asked the obvious question as to why do a lama observes such a phenomenon and was answered by equal incredulity as to why should he not! Thus, what is incredulous to us may be very obvious and commonplace to another, but if it stretches the limits of our credulity then what is to be done? On the other hand, the phenomenon of witchcraft among the Azande was explained by Evans-Pritchard by reducing the entire experience to a positivist one and subjected it to a rational positivist-functional analysis. Here, as evident, he ignored the apparent subjective experience of the actors and concentrated on the overt or even covert functions that were performed by the experiences; he took them as given conditions without comments. To him, it does not matter what the Azande felt emotionally or experientially about witchcraft. The focus of his analysis was on the role that witchcraft played in maintaining the social order. In yet some other cases the analyst, such as, Geertz (1975) emphasized on the meanings that these experiences have for the actors and then integrate the individual experiences into webs of significance. But most scientists have skirted the issue of truth of the experiences and of the "seeing" and "experiencing" of the actors. Ingold (1986) and Gell (1992), yet another category of scholars, have looked upon culture as a way of engaging with the world and the manner of this engagement is a dialectic relationship with the environment. Human beings engage with their environment forming their own interpretations as a result of this interaction and not the other way round. In other words, we do not always interact with a culturally created environment of meanings but that our physical interactions that are natural to begin with imbue the environment with meaning that then becomes transcribed into it. Such meanings, in the absence of written records, may be only partly passed down and partly recreated each time an individual engages with his/her environment. Thus, a child born into a hunter-gatherer group learns about the environment by walking in the forests, by trying to satisfy hunger by plucking fruits and catching animals and trying to survive and find its way around. There are rather complex issues facing social researchers who have to invariably deal with not only what are obvious, well known, routine matters but also with digressive activities, which we may call not normal and also not ethical. However, it is not easy to define what is ethical and normal.

To a question: what is ethical? It can be said that everything in society does not follow the same pattern. Whenever a social researcher observes actual human behaviour and activities, there are always some differences of opinion about what is right, and what is wrong? We have already discussed that the researcher is the one with any moral bias, such that what is right or wrong cannot be determined according to any particularistic principles, such as one's own value systems, but must have a universal referent. There has to be some universal criteria of well-being, such as health, life and so on, by which we may judge an action to be right or wrong. But this is a question that has continued to plague the social sciences. But by what criteria do we construct a universal code of morality or ethics? How do we reconcile the ideas of cultural relativity with transcendence of ethnocentrism? For example, anthropologists have been accused of trying to find a justification for every custom found in any society including human sacrifice and infanticide. It is still a very big question mark as to how we judge the concepts of right and wrong when they do not apply to us. As Barnes has stated;

> "The intellectual task of the natural scientist is greatly simplified because his data are, comparatively speaking, hard and reliable, and because the separation between him and the natural phenomena he studies is clear-cut. The social scientist, however deals with data that usually are unreliable and fuzzy and, more importantly, his relation to the phenomena he studies is two-sided. The people he studies not only talk, they also talk back to him. Consequently it is his kind of science, rather than that followed by the physicist or chemist, that should be called hard if we wish to indicate the difficulty of the task he faces. Certainly the small amount of success achieved so far in social science, as compared to natural science, suggests that social science is indeed a hard undertaking. Ethical problems constitute a major component of its intrinsic difficulty (1977: 2).

For the natural sciences, too, the issue of ethics remains a matter of great concern. We are all aware of ethical questions regarding weapons of mass destruction and genetic engineering. But, it is only after scientific discoveries, Laszlo and Wilbur (1970) pointed out, affect humankind that we raise ethical questions about natural sciences. Otherwise, humans as such do not figure into the theories of physics. In contrast to this situation, in the social sciences, we are dealing with human beings all the time and that is why we in social sciences have to continuously face ethical questions and it is just not possible to ignore them.

Still, the other dimension to study the social world relates to what is normative that conforms to standard, regular, usual and typical pattern. According to Durkheim, the decision of what constitutes the normal is the moot point on which social science rests (1964: 47-75). Therefore, the task is to decide what is normative and what is pathological. In the earlier phase, that is, during eighteenth and nineteenth century, of social science research, a kind of society was taken for granted that was homogeneous or everyone had the same values and norms. But, increasingly, it was realized that such a society was only the dream of ethnographers. There exists practically no human society without any differentiation and this means that for different sections of society, there may be varying values and points of view. An increasing criticism arose with the rise of the feminists and then also the subaltern and the Third-World perspectives. It was increasingly brought to the notice of the theorists that what had been portrayed as normal and regular was such only for a section of society, and even the simplest society was only the world of men. The path breaking restudy of Matinowski's field, the Trobriand Islands, by a woman anthropologist, Weiner (1976) and (1979), showed that what Malinowski had depicted as true for the entire Trobriand society was true only for the world of men. The world of women had been left out as if it did not exist, but it did and was an important dimension of life on the Trobriand Islands. Such considerations led to revision of theoretical stances including that of "multiculturalism" that has now become an important dimension of social research in the context of the global movement of people from one country to settle down in another country.

As mentioned earlier, the evolutionary social scientists had assumed that it was possible to have a universal referent to judge the normal and, more importantly, there was something that was normal as compared to the pathological. The method to go about doing so could be statistical but ultimately, as even Durkheim (1964: 53-54) realized, one had to fall back on use of deductive logic. So, for a normal social phenomenon was, we may look for its distribution in various societies of the human species, and if one kind of phenomenon is found in most communities, in spite of having variable manifestations, it may be taken as normal. To illustrate, almost all human societies have some kind of grouping we can call a family. Thus a family, of no matter what form, is usually supposed to be a normal condition of human societies and the breakdown or absence of this institution may be taken as pathological. This again indicates that there cannot be any truly objective and external conditions of normality, if normality is to be contextualized to its occurrence in different societies. Moreover, while considering distribution or occurrence in space one cannot overlook temporal distribution of a phenomenon, again raising the question that, what is normal at one point of time may not be so in other historical periods. For example, in the modern world, the term family may also denote a single parent family or a family with parents of the same sex; certainly such families would have been considered abnormal only a couple of decades back. In Durkheim's time, variability in time and space were both explained by the concept of evolution, but today history has replaced evolution, making an important difference, progress is no longer seen as an inbuilt mechanism of transformation. In fact, just as we had the concept of cultural relativity across space, the same can now be applied across time. We can truly be neutral about things that have happened and also about those that are going to happen. But as we have seen time and again such neutrality is not humanly possible about something that is occurring in the present. The acceptance of human subjectivity in the social sciences has ultimately given impetus to the emergence of the post-modern theory. Furthermore, the "logical" normality of which, Durkheim (1964: 54) spoke came under criticism as the logic of a particular observer. But Durkheim had been careful to point to the existence of "cultural relativism", to counter the "universal" laws of evolution posited by his predecessors such as Comte. He was also astute enough to separate the cause of existence of a phenomenon from its function, a teleology to which later generations of functionalists often fell.

Apart from these, the central question remains: how do we conceptualize society and culture? Unlike the natural sciences, we do not have anything concrete in front of us that we see as society or culture. What we do actually is to infer it from our observation and our assumptions. The process by which we can infer can become quite fuzzy and debatable. For example, one way in which one can refer to society as one's object of study is by its geographical definition. For example, Malinowski (1884-1942) studied in 1922 the Trobriand Islanders as a unit of study, Mead (1901-1978) studied in 1928 Samoa, Radcliffe-Brown (1881-1955) carried out his major research in 1922 among the Andaman Islanders and so on. It can be presumed that each of these field locations also contains a unique culture.

The society can also be defined in terms of some other boundary, for example, marriage. Thus, a caste or *jati* can be defined by the boundaries of endogamy. There can be other criteria of membership as well. But not all units have such boundaries; say if one wants to study a religion like Hinduism, the field would appear vast and unbounded. Sometimes what one wants to study may not be defined in one location; say a diaspora or an immigrant group that cannot be studied with reference to one location only. Even when one is bound to a location the social phenomenon need not be bounded. Thus, one cannot study a village in rural India without understanding the effects of mass media and national politics on it. Increasingly, the availability of a bounded society is being questioned and we have techniques such as multi-sited ethnographies and networks to replace the earlier concept of a system.

The term society is, repeatedly, reduced to a subjective rather than an objective unit. A society or community is one because the actors or participants define it as such. Thus, the simple way to study Hinduism would be to study those who call themselves Hindus rather than trying to devise an external definition for it. A culture could, thus, be the maximum amount of shared representations about the world that exist across a unit we call a human group. Often such a group by the very fact of sharing of representations is defined as a society. Such sharing of representations or culture is not rigid, it transforms and diffuses and transplants itself. While studying a unit of society in India, say among the youth, we cannot overlook the influence of various cultures, including that of the USA and Japan and so on. Here the task would be to separate the imposed from the original, but even such a task may become very complex, as one must take into account the historical development of ideas and interpretations of the world.

In *The Constitution of Society*, Anthony Giddens has mentioned the two primary senses of the concept of society: firstly, the generalized connotation of social association or interaction, (the standard definition that is given in the classrooms of a network or pattern of interaction between social actors); and, secondly, a relatively bounded unit of social relationships forming a system of interdependency that distinguishes it from other such systems (1984: 163). However, this was the manner in which societies were distinguished in classical times. But, today, such bounded units are hard to locate and define and increasingly it is being realized that such units may have always been an anthropologist's wishful thinking. So, what does a social scientist look for while trying to find a unit of study to be defined as a society? In some cases one may look for the boundaries of linguistic understanding, so that it becomes synonymous with a culture, or it may be a self-defined tribe, or caste or a geographical unit like a village. However, what problematizes society is its original dissociation from the individual by Durkheim (1964: 4). The social scientist in the field has to interact with and observe individuals and not society. If the individual is seen analytically opposed to society, then to make a sense of one's findings a social scientist would ignore the actor altogether and create one's own version of the structure through a process of abstraction. But if society is the product of a process of theorizing then like all theories it is contextualized in time and space. What is society then becomes itself a social activity subject to rules of power. Take for example the manner in which Indian society was defined in the colonial era by the colonial administrators with the help of social elites of India, like the Brahmins and rulers. The version of Indian society and history that was thus constructed prioritized both Brahmanism and patriarchy. Paradoxically, the constructions are not mere abstractions but if created by a source of power they translate themselves into reality and thus as social historians have been able to demonstrate, colonial rule did reconstruct Indian society into the form into which the colonials had imagined it. But in spite of this reconstruction there was a reality about society that never made it to the official version. Much later subaltern historians made attempts to salvage this history.

Considering the various problems encountered in trying to make sense of the data collected, we keep coming back to the sanctity of the term empirical reality, while dealing with the terms of society and culture. The greatest tension lies in the relationship between individual and society. The theoretical disparity remains for us to resolve regarding whether we accept the positive school, which admitted an existence of society over and above that of the individual or we merge the two in a subjective post-modernist interpretation. The status of the text as a document of reality or as a script for the subjective interaction of the observer and the observed is still a subject of debate. Even if we take the latter stand that all reality is interpretative and a form of reflexivity then also the guide for successful presentation of data would rest in the truthfulness of the representation. In fact those advocating for the latter approach accuse the positivists of imposing their own rules while systematizing the data. In other words, things have been distorted to fit into neat compartments whereas the reality is never so neat. Those who had talked about regularities and systemic patterns overlooked the validity of the irregular. In fact the definitions of the regular and irregular were tailor-made to fit into the preconceived notions of the observer. What ultimately emerge are the perceptions of the observer neatly and systematically validated by selectively presented data. Foster (1965), restudying the village of Yucatan, criticised Robert Redfield of seeing harmony and social order where the reality was fraught with suspicion, disharmony and covert conflict.

Furthermore, it may be argued that the only way is to keep as close to the observed reality as possible is to act as a mediator rather than as an interpreter of data. The present genre of social scientists especially those dealing with field realities prefer to stick as close to the narrative mode as possible, thus acting more as translators on behalf of the actors in the field. The best mode is to assume that the knowledge lies with the actors and not with the interpreters that society is what it is as a result of the interactions and activities of the actors as they engage with the world. The Durkheimian dialectic of the actor and the society is seen as more or less not valid just because society is no longer viewed as the systemic, bounded reality of shared representations as positivist scholars held it earlier. There is also an attempt to view things not only as they are but also how they came to be. Thus history has become an integral part of social science interpretations as well as power relationships and their formation. A part of power relationships is also the vantage position of the scholar, the position from which he/she speaks and represents the world. It was increasingly felt that the subject position of the scholar has been assumed to be "white" and "male" thus "othering" all those who belonged to the Third World, the Black and the Female. The word "I" used in many ethnographic narratives always invoked the male, white scholar with his western scientific rationality. For example, while almost all male white scholars looked at the world as patriarchal and male dominated, women scholars often found contra cultures where women had their own modes and ways of countering male domination and their own strengths and voices. Contrarily, men often missed out on forms and manners of oppression that were visible to women. This is only one example, others can be of studies of the caste system from the bottom up, studies of feminism from the perspective of black women, studies of indigenous people by indigenous scholars and so on.

However, the problem has been partially solved by the concept of relational objectivity or relationalism. In this the social scientist makes clear at the outset, the perspective that is being followed in the analysis so that readers can subsequently put in the context the findings and draw their own conclusions. The point is to make clear the basic assumptions on which the theory is formulated and it is for other scholars to accept or reject the theory on the basis of whether the basic premises are acceptable or not. For example, the entire debate on whether matriarchy or patriarchy was the initial stage of human society is meaningful only when one accepts the basic premise of the stage-by-stage evolution of human societies. If one does not accept the basic premise itself, then the entire debate becomes meaningless. If we do not accept the above path, the only generalizations that can have universal validity in the social sciences are the statistical generalizations, for example, the fact that female infanticide rates have increased from 1950 to 2020. But such generalizations are not theory. They only form the basis for theory and when a theory is formulated out of statistical generalizations there is still plenty of scope for varied interpretations.

Finally, because researchers' background skills are internal in relation to their activity, ethnomethodologists contend that researchers must explicitly account for their procedures in producing knowledge. This is seen by the ethnomethodologists as especially important in the study of society, because here researchers' production of knowledge is an important part of human activity and can therefore not be left out as study object (Garfinkel 1984: 33). It is precisely here that the ethnomethodologists see a breakdown in the possibility for objective social sciences. A formalization and theorization of the researchers' background skills into genuine rules of research is thus necessary for this objectivity, say the ethnomethodologists. However, such formalization is not possible because the researchers' basic skills are situational. Infinite regress again sticks up its ugly head: how does one formalize the skills, which make formalization possible? (Flyvbjerg 2001: 34)

The acquisition of researchers' basic skills is no different from acquisition of other skills. Researchers do not need to be able to formulate rules for their skills in order to practice them with success.

On the contrary, studies show that rules can obstruct the continuous exercise of high-level skills. There is nothing which indicates that researchers at expert level – those who have achieved genuine mastery in their field – use mainly context-independent rules or traditional rationality in their best scientific performances, even though they might depict it as such when they get around to writing their scholarly articles or memoirs. The same is true for other professionals: clever businessmen, eminent doctors, pilots with "the right stuff," inspiring teachers, instinctual financiers, skilled shoemakers, and prize-winning journalists. And this use of tacit skills instead of rules also applies to everyday activities. Anthony Giddens could benefit here from using the concept "practical consciousness" which he has developed in another context, to reinforce his double hermeneutic and the hermeneutic-phenomenological argument, but apparently has not. He defines "practical consciousness" as "all the things which actor knows tacitly about how to 'go on' in the context of social life without being able to give them direct discursive expression" (1984: xxii). It is precisely the kind of "tacit skills" referred to by Giddens and others which characterizes the highest levels of the learning process. Tacit skills are that level on which expert researchers operate.

Opposed to this view stands the rationalist view, which builds upon Plato's and Kant's theories that the human brain works on the basis of rules. Skills are therefore seen as rule-based, and development from beginner to expert level is explained in terms of the development of more and better rules. Whereas the beginner uses the rules consciously, the expert uses them unconsciously, but in the rationalist view both are instances of rule-based behaviour (Flyvbjerg 2001: 35). No genuine proof exists as to the validity of either the hermeneutic or the rationalist view. Introspection does not help, in that both camps agree that regardless of what happens with human experts, it happens unconsciously. Existing experiments do not clearly point in one or the other direction. However, the documented failure of cognitivism and artificial intelligence to simulate human intelligence on the basis of rules can be taken as an indication of the limitations of the rationalist view. The attempts to develop artificial intelligence can in this sense be seen as the litmus test of the two views. The cognitivists' project's lack of success when faced with the Dreyfus model's ability to account for the transition to the effortless, intuitive performance of experts means that on empirical and practical grounds, we must currently opt for the Dreyfus model over the cognitive model. For the moment, then, we must assume that the researchers' basic skills, as with other high-level skills, cannot be described theoretically in terms of objective rules. And inasmuch as the study of human affairs, according to the ethnomethodologists, requires such a description in order to become normal science, it follows that the social sciences are incapable of achieving scientific status in this sense.

Conclusion

There have, of course, been numerous general theories of history or society whose thinkers have claimed for them the validity of science. The fact is, however, that what have been claimed as sciences of society have never turned out to be more than philosophies of human history. This applies to the various eighteenth-century attempts to found sciences of morals and history, including Marxism, despite the claim made by Engels at Marx's graveside that 'just as Darwin discovered the law of development of organic nature, so Marx discovered the law of development.' But to start by looking for a general theory of society is likely to remain in social science research. In practice, the most important problem which follows from the nature of the social science research is one which can be very simply put by Weber. He persistently and correctly emphasizes that there can be no definitive vocabulary for the analysis of social phenomena. Even the concept of 'culture' is a 'value-concept.' There are no positivistic criteria on which the choice can be made.

There are, of course, a number of other objections which have been raised in denial of the possibility of social science to idealize science. These, however, are of a less fundamental character and can be treated (as by the positivists) as technical. It is denied, for instance, that we can ever generalize about human affairs, because of the impossibility of conducting historical experiments. But this is equally true of astronomy or geology, and these two branches of learning are not normally denied a claim to science. It is true that historical sequences are unique in a further and different sense which does not apply to the movement of planets or the shrinkage of the crust of the earth. It is sometimes said of social research that it involves too many variables to make scientific procedure possible. "Any prediction made by social scientists is about people who can by their conscious action upset the prediction made" (Simon, 1957: 82-3). So it is rightly said by Runciman, an eminent social scientist, "The proper function of a social science is not prediction but diagnosis" (1969: 17).

The commonest type of objection which is liable to be levelled against social science is that they are all concerned with people, and people are apt, quite naturally, to have ideas of their own about how and why they and other people in general behave. They have, thus, a standard rejoinder with which they can confront any proposition advanced by a social scientist: if they agree with it, it is obvious; if they disagree with it, it is wrong. Whichever of two contradictory but, of course, obvious propositions of this kind is found on systematic inquiry to be correct, there will always be somebody to maintain that he knew it all beforehand. What the social researcher has to do is to establish which of two contradictory truisms is correct, and to what extent and under what conditions it holds good. The only way to do this is to follow as far as possible, given the necessary reservations, the procedures of scientific method.

This leaves, finally, only the most general and speculative question: how far is social science likely to progress? To try too hard to offer an answer to this is not only a difficult undertaking but a foolish one, for anyone who knew would, as it were, be there already. Nobody has yet successfully produced a general theory of societies, and it is hard not so doubt whether anybody ever will. A significant advance has still to be made in the social science research in the large, uncertain and difficult area where psychological factors interact or overlap with social. When our subject-matter is people, their collective behaviour has to be explained by reference to factors both inside and outside of them. The problem which therefore confronts the social researchers is that of trying to formulate in a particular area of behaviour some general propositions about the conditions under which a proportional influence should be assigned to each type of variable. Prediction, as cannot be too much emphasized, is never enough. Of course, we can predict elections, or formulate economic policies, or estimate population trends because we can treat such questions in the aggregate.

In making assertions about the relevant systems (or sets of variables), we can assume that individual differences are being randomized out, just as an engineer can build a bridge by calculations of size or stress without taking account of the individual molecular occurrences of which his bridge is actually made. But the social scientist, even when he has discovered the most consistent correlations between aggregate data, has not given a full explanation until the personal factors of character and temperament have been assigned their relative weight. Attempts have been made with moderate success to correlate political behaviour with psychological as opposed to social factors. But we are a very long way from even an approximate estimate of the relative importance of the one as opposed to the other. It must be possible, at least, that a real advance may be made in this direction; or, to state it more cautiously still, if such an advance is about to be made it is likely to prove an exceedingly important one. However, this is not to say that it is impossible to make interesting generalizations about political behaviour and to test these by methods modelled, at least, on those of natural science. It is only to say, if you like, that though all sciences are sciences some will always remain more scientific than others; nor is there really any reason why even the partisans of social science should find this distressing.

From the perspective of critics in the naturalist tradition, social science is bad science, or immature science. The research in social science faced the shortcomings, such as, thinness of data, the crudeness of methods, the inexactness of findings, lack of precision, inconsistency and indeterminacy, lack of progress and cumulation, lack of unifying theory, lack of objectivity and neutrality. Furthermore, it is being argued that there is too much of impressionistic narrative in the work of social science research, too much rhetoric, and not enough scientific ballast. For humanist, social science is in a condition of permanent paradigmatic revolution which is not due to poor execution and insufficient rigour, but because of the impossibility of the naturalist ideal. They argued that the problems encountered in a social science focussed on human actions and institutions are quite different from those encountered in a science focussed on inanimate objects, mathematical regularities, and genetically programmed behaviour. They put forward that the social sciences have a harder task cut out for them. For them, the methods useful for investigating human action and the sorts of question a social researcher are inclined to ask are quite different from those applied to the study of nature. And, still, in the contemporary social science this leaves open the possibility that we could still apply the natural science model, even if only imperfectly. Further, it is overtly quantitative, obsessed with abstract model that have few real-life applications. Also, it is too limited in scope, leaving out normative questions so that the social sciences are equated with quasi-sciences and quasi-humanities.

As far as the knowledge of human society was concerned, the philosophy of the Enlightenment gave a new direction. For them, 'society exists out there readily amenable to empirical observation.' This knowledge of society can be objective and universal, and hence cumulative and progressive; different from and superior to ideological distortions and religious beliefs; and, positively useful for the restructuring of human society. The writings of the Enlightenment philosophers, as discussed earlier, profoundly affected politics and the development of social research. The French Revolution (1789) and the American Revolution (1776) had many causes but many Enlightenment ideas and ways of thinking had a great effect on these political and social changes. The slogans of "liberty, equality, fraternity" and "life, liberty and pursuit of happiness" state the political ideals of these revolutions and reflect the ideas of *philosophes*. Thus, we have tried to understand the philosophical bases of the social research and how different epistemological and metaphysical issues dealt within philosophy have had a bearing on various perspectives and methodologies of the social sciences.

All of us attach a special status to the notion of scientific knowledge because it depicts the world as it is rather than as anyone of us may wish it to be. In this sense scientific knowledge provides us the possibility of gaining a true understanding of the nature of the social and natural world. Positivism emerged at a time when sociological study was trying to establish itself as a science. And positivism continues to have its appeal. We have discussed the antecedents of positivism in the context of tremendous strides made in the sciences and of the general milieu of Enlightenment. Auguste Comte is considered the founder of sociology for he tried to conceive of similar methodology for the social sciences and the study of society. Positivism, as we can see, had a tremendous impact on sociology and in some ways helped establish it as a discipline. The propositions and theories of Comte have, however, been refined especially in the case of Durkhiem. He, by far, has been responsible for defining the subject matter of sociology and in laying out the rules to study society. Subsequent thinkers have critiqued his visualization of an overarching coercive society, but Durkhiem still lays out a road map for us to follow and be clear in distinguishing individual acts from societal acts. But then, with the passage of time, with new experiences leading to disillusionment with the so called 'neutrality' of science, and with new sensitivity to reflexivity and creativity, we see the growing critique of positivism. The subsequent methodologies and perspectives in sociology attempted to privilege the agency of the individual. We have discussed Giddens' work as an example of this approach. Another critique that came strongly against positivism came from Gouldner, who felt that positivism with its methodological coldness separates the knower from the known and, therefore, he pleads for a reflexive sociology. Many in the social sciences, especially in social anthropology, have recommended reflexiveness. The issues of who represents whoever has come under severe debate not only in anthropology but also in the general debates in the social sciences. With the post-modernist critique of unilinear theories there is an increasing tendency to look for multi-vocality. The question that can be asked in this context is what relevance do theories, which support generalizing tendencies, have in the globalizing world? These debates and contestations have enriched the discipline. And it is important that we become aware of these multiple voices within the discipline. Hence, there has been no single paradigm or theory which has dominated the social research. Though it was influenced by natural science and its methodologies, especially in its early stages, in an attempt to establish itself as a discipline, it has realized that the subject matter of social research, involving as it is human beings, is not amenable to generalizations and laws of the Newtonian kind. With the discovery of increasingly different worldviews and particular cultures, it became difficult for social researchers to come up with universal explanations. Even if they did, the same came under heavy criticism. Hence, the increasing need to represent plurality has produced a new wave of critique leading to a post-modernist's valorization of many methods and in that almost everything is acceptable.

Where do we go after the basis itself for knowledge as an objective quest for truth is subject to questioning? Well, not all social scientists converted to post-modernism even when they came face-to-face with the problems of modernity and science. Most enriching have been the debates on critiques of positivism leading to the development of reflexive sociology and an alternative sociology dealing with the creativity of the social actor. Now the social scientist is actually concerned with what you and I think and do. That makes the subjects under the social sciences umbrella very interesting indeed. Once you and I find place in the scope of a subject like social science, we are able to participate in not only understanding the social reality around us but also changing it through our conscious efforts.

Finally, the term "science" is hard to define. It comprises many different aspects of learning. It involves making observations about nature and designing experiments; and, making conclusions and trying to better understand the world me live in. Broadly speaking, it is a systematic way to study the world in which we live involving several systematic steps for the process of scientific inquiry. These include: making scientific observations; proposing scientific questions; designing scientific experiments; collecting scientific information; making scientific interpretations; evaluating scientific assumptions; discussing scientific implications; and evaluating different point of views. Today's modern science is really a combination of science as ideas, science as discovery, and science as invention. Science as ideas we now call philosophy; science as discovering we call a particular scientific discipline, such as chemistry, or biology; and science as invention, we call technology. Researchers use systematic or particular methods, such as observation and experimentation, to give a better understanding of the world around us. They collect information or data; then they use this data to make conclusions and predictions about how the world works. They also use instrumentation to help them make observations that they will observe with their senses alone. Furthermore, the basis of a scientific knowledge is its objectivity, that is, the use of facts without distortion by personal feelings or prejudices; encourage the methods that eliminate the subjective by limiting choices to fixed alternatives; to express the nature of reality as it is, not being governed by personal reflections or feelings; and to be observable or verifiable especially by scientific methods. In other words, objectivity relates to expressing or involving the use of facts without distortion by present feelings or prejudices and in this sense referring to methods that eliminate the subjective by limiting choices to fixed alternatives requiring a minimum of creative interpretation. If also refers to emphasising or expressing the nature of reality as it is apart from personal reflections or feelings and therefore belonging to the sensible world and being observable or verifiable especially by scientific methods.

Bibliography

Aberle, D.F. 1950, "The Functional Prerequisites of a Society," *Ethics,* vol. LX, no. 2, January.

Ashby, W. Ross 1956, *An Introduction to Cybernetics* (New York: J. Wiley).

Bacon, Francis 1970, "On the Interpretations of Nature and the Empire of Man" in J.E. Curtis and J. W. Petras, The Sociology of knowledge: A Reader (London: Duckworth).

Barnes, J. A. 1977, *The Ethics of Inquiry in Social Science* (New Delhi: Oxford University Press).

Barth, Frederick 1987, *Cosmology in the Making: A Generative Approach to Cultural Variations in inner New Guinea* (Cambridge: Cambridge University Press).

Baudrillard, J. 1983, *In the Shadow of the Silent Majorities* (New York: The MIT Press).

Bernstein, J. Richard 1985, *Beyond Objectivism and Relativism: Science, Hermeneutics, and Praxis* (Pennsylvania: University of Pennsylvania Press).

Bhabha, Jacqueline 2003, "Children, Migration and International Norms" in T. A. Aleinikoff and V. Chetail (eds.) *Migration and International Legal Norms* (The Hague: T. M. C. Asser Press).

Bell, D. (1976), *The Cultural Contradictions of Capitalism* (London: Routledge).

Blumer, Herbert 1937, "Social Psychology," in E. Schmidt (eds.) *Man and Society* (New York: Prentice-Hall).

Blumer, Herbert 1962, "Society and Symbolic Interaction" in Arnold M.

Rose (ed.) *Human Behavior and Social Process* (Boston: Houghton Mifflin).

Blumer Herbert 1969, *Symbolic Interactionism: Perspective and Method* (New Jersey: Prentice-Hall, Englewood Cliffs).

Braybrooke, David 1987, *Philosophy of Social Science* (New Jersey: Prentice-Hall, Englewood Cliffs).

Bryant, C. G. A. 1985, *Positivism in Social Theory and Research* (London: Macmillan).

Castaneda, Carlos 1971, *A Separate Reality* (Harmondsworth: Penguin Books).

Chapin, F. Stuart 1963, "The Social Effects of Public Housing in Minnepolis" in Matilda White Riley (ed.), *Sociological Research: A Case Approach,* Vol. I (New York and Burlingame: Harcourt Brace and World Inc).

Clark, Ronald 1982, *Freud: The Man and the Cause* (London: Granada).

Collingwood, R.G. 1946, *The Idea of History* (Oxford: Oxford University Press).

Comte, Auguste (1830-42), *Course of Positive Philosophy*. Six Volumes, reprint in 2001 (New Jersey: Thoemmes Press).

Comte, Auguste (1851-54), *System of Positive Philosophy*, reprinted in 1961 (New York: Calvin Blanchard).

Coser, Lewis A. 1956, *The Functions of Social Conflict* (New York: The Free Press).

Dahrendorf, Ralf G. 1959, *Class and Conflict in Industrial Society* (Stanford: Stanford University Press).

Descartes, Rene 1641, *Meditations on the First Philosophy* (English translation published in 1991 by Cottingham, Stoothoff, Murdoch and Kenny).

Dilthey, Wilhelm 1883, *Introduction to Human Sciences* (Princeton: Princeton University Press).

Du Bois 1983, "Passionate Scholarship: Notes on Values, Knowing and Method in Feminist Social Science," in G.Bowles and R. Duelli-Kiein (ed.) *Theories of Women's Studies* (London: Routledge and Kegan Paul).

Durant, W. 1961, *Story of Philosophy* (New York: Pocket Books).

Durkheim, Emile 1964, *The Division of Labour in Society,* published in 1991 (New York: The Free Press).

Durkheim, Emile 1964, (first published in 1895), *The Rules of Sociological Method* (New York: The Free Press)

Edie, James M. 1967, "Transcendental Phenomenology and Existentialism" in Joseph J. Kockelmans (ed.) *Phenomenology: The Philosophy of Edmund Husserl and Its Interpretation* (New York: Doubleday Anchor Books).

Eisenstein, Zillah 1979, *Capitalist Patriarchy and the Case for Socialist Feminism* (New York: Monthly Review Press).

Elster, John 1989, *Nuts and Bolts of Social Research* (Cambridge: Cambridge University Press).

Epstein, Scarlet 1979, "Mysore Village Revisited" in G. M. Foster, T. Scudder, E. Colson, R. V. Kemper (eds.) *Long-term Field Research in Social Anthropology* (Orlando, New York, London: Academic Press).

Evans-Pritchard, E. E. 1937, *Witchcraft, Oracles and Magic among the Azande* (Oxford: Clarendon Press).

Fergusson, Wallace K. and Geoffrey Brunn 1958, *A Survey of European Civilization* (Boston: Houston Mifflin Company).

Ferree, Myra Max, Judieth Lorber and Beth B. Heiss 1999, *Revisioning Gender* (Thousand Oaks: Sage Publication).

Feyerabend, Paul 1982, *Science in a Free Society* (London: Verso).

Flyvbjerg, Bent 2001, *Making Social Science Matter* (Cambridge: Cambridge University Press).

Focault, Michel 1973, *The Order of Things: An Archaeology of Human Sciences* (New York: Vintage).

Foster, George M. 1965, "Peasant Society and the image of the limited Good," *American Anthropologist,* 67:293-315.

Freud, Sigmund 1950, "Project for a Scientific Psychology," in *The Standard Edition of the Cambridge Psychological Works of Sigmund Freud,* vol.I (London: Hograth Press).

Friedman, Jonathan 2004, "PostModernism" in Adam Kuper and Jessica Kuper (ed.) *The Social Science Encyclopaedia*, volume II, third edition (New York: Routledge).

Foster, George M. 1965, "Peasant Society and the Image of the Limited Good," *American Anthropologist*, 67:293-315.

Gadamer, Hans-Georg 1985, "Truth and Method" in Mueller-Vollmer Kurt (ed.) *The Hermeneutics Reader: Texts of the German Tradition from the Enlightenment to the Present* (New York: Crossroad).

Garfinkel, Harold 1984, *Studies in Ethnomethodology* (Cambridge: Polity Press).

Geertz, Clifford 1975, *Thick Description: Toward an Interpretative Theory of Culture* in The Interpretation of Cultures: Selected Essays Clifford Geertz (London: Hutchinson).

Geertz, Clifford 1983, *Local Knowledge* (New York: Basic).

Gell, Alfred 1992, *The Anthropology of Time: Cultural Construction of Temporal Maps and Imagers* (Oxford: Berg Publishers).

Gerring, John 2001, *Social Science Methodology: A Critical Framework* (Cambridge: Cambridge University Press).

Giddens, Anthony 1982, "Hermeneutics and Social Theory," in *Profiles and Critiques in Social Theory* (CA: University of California Press, Berkeley).

Giddens, Anthony 1981, "Phenomenology" in Duncan G Mitchell (ed.) *A New Dictionary of Sociology* (London: Routledge & Kegan Paul).

Giddens, Anthony 1984, *The Constitution of Society: Outline of the Theory of Structuralism* (Cambridge: Polity Press).

Giddens, Anthony 1987, *Social Theory and Modern Sociology* (Cambridge: Polity Press).

Giddens, Anthony 1990, *The Consequences of Modernity* (London: Polity Press).

Gorelick, Sherry 1991, "Contradictions in Feminist Methodology," *Gender and Society* 5(4).

Gouldner, Alvin W. 1970, *The Coming Crisis of Western Sociology* (London: Heinemann).

Habermas, J. 1985, "Hermeneutics and the Social Sciences" in Mueller-Vollmer Kurt (ed.). *The Hermeneutics Reader: Texts of the German Tradition from the Enlightenment to the Present* (New York: Crossroad).

Habermas, J. 1987, *The Philosophical Discourse of Modernity* (Cambridge, MA.: The MIT Press).

Hamspshire, Stuart 1959, *Thought and Action* (Michigan: Chatto and Windus).

Harding, Sandra (ed.) 1987, *Feminism and Methodology: Social Science Issues* (Bloomington: Indiana University Press).

Harvey, D. (1990), *The Condition of Postmodernity* (Oxford: Blackwell Publishers).

Hekman, Susan J. 1986, *Hermeneutics and the Sociology of Knowledge*, (Cambridge: Polity Press).

Hempel, Carl G. 1942, *Philosophy of Natural Science* (New Jersey: Prentice-Hall, Englewood Cliffs).

Hensman, Rohini 2005, "Revolutionizing the Family," *Economic and Political Weekly*, XL (8): 709-712.

Herbert A. Simon 1957, *Models of Man: Social and Rational* (New York: John Wiley and Sons, Inc.).

Holmswood, John and Alexander Stewart 1991, *Explanation and Social Theory* (London: Mcmillan).

Homan, George C. 1950, *The Human Group* (New York: Harcourt Brace and World).

Husserl, Edmund 1913 (translated in 1931), *Ideas: A General Introduction to Pure Phenomenology* (The Hague: Nijhoff).

Husserl Edmund 1950, *Cartesian Meditations*, S. Strasser, Husserliana (ed.), Vol.1 (The Hague: Martinus Nijhoff).

Husserl, Edmund 1965, "Philosophy as Rigorous Science" in *Phenomenology and the Crisis of Philosophy,* translated by Quentin Lauer (New York: Harper Torchbooks).

Ingold, Tim 1986, *Evolution and Social Life* (Cambridge: Cambridge University Press).

John, Mary E. 2003, "The Encounter of Women's Studies and Sociology: Questions from the Borders" in Maitrayee Chaudhari (ed.). *The Practice of Sociology* (New Delhi: Orient Longman).

John, Mary E. 2005, "Feminist Perspective on Family and Marriage," *Economic and Political Weekly*, XL (8): 712-715.

Johnson, Christopher 2004, "Structuralism" in *The Social Science Encyclopaedia*, volume II third edition, Adam Kuper, and Jessica Kuper (ed.) (New York: Routledge).

Johnson, Miriam 1991, "Feminism and the Theories of Talcott Parsons" in Ruth A. Wallace (ed.). *Feminism and Sociological Theory* (London: Sage Publications).

Kincaid, Harold 1990, "Defending Laws in Social Sciences," *Philosophy of Social Sciences* 20: 56-83.

Kloos, Peter 2004, "Restudies in Anthropology" in V. K. Srivastava (ed.). *Methodology and Fieldwork* (New Delhi: Oxford University Press).

Krishnaraj, Maithreyi 2005, "Research on Women Studies: Need for a Critical Appraisal," *Economic and Political Weekly* XL (28): 2008-2017.

Kuhn, Thomas S. 1970, *The Structure of Scientific Revolution* (Chicago: University of Chicago Press).

Kuhn, Thomas S. 1977, *The Essential Tensions: Selected Studies in Scientific Traditions and Change* (Chicago: University of Chicago Press).

Kuhn, Thomas S. 1987, "What Are Scientific Revolutions," in Lorenz Kruger, Lorraine J. Daston, and Michael Heidelberger (ed.). *The Probabilistic Revolution: Ideas in History,* vol. 1 (Cambridge: MIT Press).

Lash, S. and Urry, J. (1987), *The End of Organized Capitalism* (Oxford: Polity Press).

Laszlo, Ervin and James Benjamin Wilbur 1970, *Human Values and Natural Science: Proceedings of the Third Conference on Value Inquiry*, Current Topics of Contemporary Thought, vol. 4 (New York: Gordan and Breach).

Little, Daniel 1991, *Varieties of Social Explanation: An Introduction to the Philosophy of Social Science* (Boulder, Colorado: Westview Press).

Little, Daniel 1992, "On the Scope and limits of Generalizations in the Social Sciences," *Boston Colloquium for the Philosophy of Science*, Boston University.

Lyotard, J.F. (1984 [1979]), *The Postmodern Condition: A Report on Knowledge* (Minneapolis: University of Minnesota).

Madan, Triloki Nath 2004, "In Pursuit of Anthropology" in V. K. Srivastava (ed.). *Methodology and Fieldwork* (New Delhi: Oxford University Press).

Martindale, Don 1960, *The Nature and Types of Sociological Theory* (Boston: Houghton Mifflin).

Marx, Karl 1975, *Early Writings* (Harmondsworth: Penguin Books).

Mazlish, Bruce 1998, *The Uncertain Sciences* (New Haven: Yale University Press).

Merton, Robert K. 1968, *Social Theory and Social Structure,* enlarged edition (New York: The Free Press).

McIntyre Alisdair 1973, "Is a Science of Comparative Politics Possible?" in A. Ryan (ed.). *The Philosophy of Social Explanation* (Oxford: Oxford University Press).

McIntyre Lee, 1991, *Problems in the Philosophy of Social Science: Towards a Defense of Nomological Explanation in the Social Science,* Ph.D. Dissertation, University of Michigan.

McCloskey, Donald 1990, *If You Are So Smart* (Chicago: Chicago University Press).

Mill, James Stuart 1930, *A System of Logic* (New York: Longmans).

Mitchell, Duncan G. 1981, *A New Dictionary of Sociology* (London: Routledge & Kegan Paul).

Mudimbe, V. Y. and Bogumil Jewsiewicki, eds. 1996, *Open the Social Sciences: Report of the Gulbekian Commission on the the Restructuring of the Social Sciences* (Stanford, CA: Stanford University Press).

Murdock, G. P. 1975, *Outline of World Culture,* Human Relations Area Files: New Haven.

Myres, K. A. et. al. 1998, *Feminist Foundation: Toward Transforming Sociology* (London: Sage Publication).

Nagel, Ernest 1971, *The Structure of Science: Problems in the Logic of Scientific Explanation* (London: Routledge and Kegan Paul).

Needham, Rodney 1963, Introduction, in Durkheim, Emile 1963 (first published in 1903)., *Primitive Classification,* translated by Rodney Needham, (Chicago: The University of Chicago Press).

Nisbet, Robert 1967, *The Sociological Tradition* (London: Heinemann).

Osborne, R. 1991, *Philosophy for Beginners* (New York: Writers and Readers).

Palmer, R.E. 1969, *Hermeneutics: Interpretation Theory in Schleiermacher, Dilthey, Heidegger and Gadamer* (IL: Evanston).

Parsons, Talcott 1937, *The Structure of Social Action* (New York: McGraw Hill).

Parsons, Talcott 1951, *The Social System* (New York: The Free Press).

Parsons, Talcott 1966, *Societies: Evolutionary and Comparative Perspectives* (New Jersey: Prentice-Hall, Englewood Cliffs).

Parsons, Talcott 1967, *Sociological Theory and Modern Society* (New York: The Free Press).

Peters, E. L. 1981, "Structuralism" in Duncan G Mitchell (ed.). *A New Dictionary of Sociology* (London: Routledge & Kegan Paul).

Popper, Karl 1957, *The Open Society and its Enemies* (London: Routledge).

Popper, Karl 1961, *The Poverty of Historicism* (London: Routledge).

Popper, Karl 1972, *Conjectures and Refutation: The Growth of Scientific Knowledge* (London: Routledge and Kegan Paul).

Pouillon, Jean 2004, "Claude Levi-Strauss" in Adam Kuper and Jessica Kuper (ed.). *The Social Science Encyclopaedia*, volume II, 3rd. edition (NY: Routledge).

Quine, Willard von Orman 1953, "Two Dogmas of Empiricism," in *From A Logical Point of View* (Cambridge, MA: Harvard University Press).

Radcliffe-Brown, A. R. 1952, *Structure and Function in Primitive Society* (London: Cohen and West).

Rao, Anupama 2005, "Sexuality and Family Form," *Economic and Political Weekly*, XL (8): 715-718.

Raymond, Aaron 1965, *Main Currents in Sociological Thought*. 2 vols. (Harmondsworth: Penguin Books).

Rege, Sharmila (ed.) 2003, *Sociology of Gender: The Challenge of Feminist Sociological Knowledge* (New Delhi: Sage).

Ricoeur, Paul 1973, "The Model of Text: Meaningful Action Considered as a Text," *New Literary History*, vol. 5, no.1, Autumn.

Ritzer, George 1983, *Sociological Theory* (New York: Alfred A. Knopf).

Robertson, Roland 1981, "Functionalism" in Duncan G Mitchell (ed.). *A New Dictionary of Sociology* (London: Routledge & Kegan Paul).

Rorty, Richard 1979, *Philosophy and the Mirror of Nature* (Princeton: Princeton University Press).

Rosaldo, Renato 1984, "Grief and a Head Hunter's Rage" in Edward Bruner (ed.). *Text, Play and Story*, The 1983 Proceedings of the American Ethnological Society: Washington D. C.

Rudner, Richard 1966, Philosophy of Social Science (New Jersey: Prentice-Hall, Englewood Cliffs).

Runciman, W.G. 1969, *Social Science and Political Theory* (Cambridge: Cambridge University Press).

Sahlins, Marshalls 1976, *Culture and Practical Reasons* (Chicago: University of Chicago).

Scholte, Jan Aart 2000, "What is Globalization? The Definitional Issue-Again" CSGR Working Paper No. 109/02, University of Warwick, December.

Schutz, Alfred 1967, *The Problem of Social Reality*, Collected Papers, vol.1 (The Hague: Martinus Nijhoff).

Scott, James C. 1998, *Seeing Like a State: How Certain Schemes to Improve the Human Condition Have Failed* (New Haven: Yale University Press).

Shostak, Marjorie 1981, *Nisa: the Life and Words of a Kung Woman* (Cambridge: Harvard University Press, Mass).

Simmel, George 1898, "The Persistence of Social Groups," *American Journal of Sociology*, 3: 829-836.

Simon, Herbert A. 1957, *Models of Man* (New York: Wiley).

Sperber, Dan 1982, *On Anthropological Knowledge* (Cambridge: Cambridge University Press).

Spiegelberg Herbert 1969, *The Phenomenological Movement*, vol.1 (The Hague: Martinus Nijhoff).

Sorokin, Pitrim A. 1962 (originally pubkished in 1937-41). *Social and Cultural Dynamics* (New Jersey: The Bedminister Press, Totowa).

Sorokin, Pitrim A. 1966, *Sociological Theory Today* (New York: Harper & Row).

Srinivas, M.N. 1976, *The Remembered Village* (Berkeley: University of California Press).

Stacey, Judith and Barri Thorne 1998, "The Missing Feminist Revolution in Sociology," in K.A. Myres, C. D. Anderson and B. J. Risman (eds.). *Feminist Foundation: Toward Transforming Sociology* (New York: Sage Publications).

Stiglitz, Joseph E. 2002, *Globalization and Its Discontents* (New York and London: Norton).

Thompson, John B. 1987, *Critical Hermeneutics: A Study in the Thought of Paul Ricoeur and J. Habermas* (Cambridge: Cambridge University Press).

Thompson, John B. 2004, "Hermeneutics," in Adam Kuper and Jersica Kuper (ed.). *The Social Science Encyclopaedia*, volume II third edition (London and New York: Routledge).

Turner, Bryan (ed.). 2000, *The Blackwell Companion of Social Theory* (Oxford: Basil Blackwell).

Turner, Victor 1971, *Dramas, Fields and Metaphors: Symbolic Action in Human Society* (New York: Cornell University Press, Ithaca).

Waters, Malcolm 1994, *Modern Sociological Theory* (London: Sage).

Weber, Max *The Theory of Social and Economic Organization* (New York: Oxford University Press).

Weber, Max 1949, *The Methodology of the Social Sciences* (New York: Free Press).

Weinberg, Steven 1998, "The Revolution that didn't Happen", *The New York Review of Books*, October 8.

Weiner, Annette B. 1976, *Women of Value, Men of Renown* (Austin and London: University of Texas Press).

Weiner, Annette B. 1979, *Trobriand Kinship from Another View: The Reproductive Power of Women and Men*, Man (NS). 14: 328-348.

White, Leslie Alvin 1945, "Diffusion versus Evolution: An Anti-Evolutionist Fallacy," *American Anthropologist* 47.

White, Leslie Alvin 1947, "Evolutionary Stages, Progress and the Evaluation of Cultures," *Southwestern Journal of Anthropology,* 3.

White, Leslie Alvin 1959, "The Expansion of the Scope of Science," in Morton H. Fried, Readings (ed.). *Anthropology*, vol.1 (New York: Crowell).

Williams, Robin 1981, "Symbolic Interactionism" in Duncan G Mitchell (ed.). *A New Dictionary of Sociology* (London: Routledge & Kegan Paul).

Windelband Wilhelm 1914, *A History of Philosophy,* published in 1964 (New York: Image Books).

Yolton, John W. 2004, John Locke (1632-1704). in Adam Kuper and Jersica Kuper (ed.). *The Social Science Encyclopaedia*, volume II third edition (London and New York: Routledge).

Zald, Mayer 1991, "Sociology as a Discipline: Quasi-Science and Quasi-Humanities," in *The American Sociologists, 22.*

Zeitlin, Irving M. 1987, *Rethinking Sociology,* first Indian edition (New Delhi: Rawat Publications).

Zeitlin, Irving M. 1990, *Ideology and the Development of Sociological Thought*, Fourth edition (New Jersey: Prentice Hall, Englewood Cliffs).

Zetterberg, Hans L. 1965, *On Theory and Verification* (New Jersey: The Bedminister Press, Totowa).

Index